Beyond Photography

Encounters with orbs, angels and mysterious light-forms!

KATIE HALL AND JOHN PICKERING

First published by O Books, 2006
An imprint of John Hunt Publishing Ltd.,
The Bothy,
Deershot Lodge,
Park Lane,
Ropley, Hants,
SO24 0BE, UK
office1@o-books.net
www.o-books.net

USA and Canada
NBN
custserv@nbnbooks.com
Tel: 1 800 462 6420 Fax: 1 800 338 4550

Australia
Brumby Books
sales@brumbybooks.com
Tel: 61 3 9761 5535 Fax: 61 3 9761 7095

Singapore
STP
davidbuckland@tlp.com.sg
Tel: 65 6276 Fax: 65 6276 7119

South Africa
Alternative Books
altbook@global.co.za
Tel: 27 011 792 7730 Fax: 27 011 972 7787

Design: Stuart Davies

ISBN-13: 978 1 905047 90 1
ISBN-10: 1 905047 90 8

A CIP catalogue record for this book is available from the British Library.

Printed in the US by Maple Vail

Beyond Photography

Encounters with orbs, angels
and mysterious light-forms!

KATIE HALL AND JOHN PICKERING

BOOKS

Winchester, UK
Washington, USA

Acknowledgements

We would like to thank our family and friends for their encouragement and support, especially; Wendy and Dave, Annabel, George, Mike, Fran, Sam and Mabel for their participation as fellow 'orb hunters'; and Brian Sibley for his critical appraisal. Our thanks also to, our publishers; John Hunt and O-Books, for all their expertise and help. And we would also like to thank Tony Dodd and all those who have shared their individual insights and experiences with us of their own journeys along the oft hidden paths to unknown horizons.

Lastly we give our thanks to all our visiting luminosities and light-forms; without whose consistent appearances and inspiration, we could not have written this book.

CONTENTS

PREFACE

I don't know who you are, dear reader, but one thing I do know is that you haven't picked up this book by chance. There is no such thing as chance. Nor are you alone; even if there is no one else in sight. Woven through our familiar everyday world is a realm of the unseen and unknown. How do I know this? If you wish to find out, you must join us for a journey into the beyond.

But before we begin our adventure together, let us give you a brief idea of who we are and where we may be heading.

While working through the text and images for this book on the computer, an odd thing happened. The mouse began to move all by itself on the mouse pad, clicking open folders and files and then, obligingly, closing them down again! I sat back and waited for this display of curiosity to subside. A few moments later all was back to normal and I had the computer to myself again. Four years ago we would have found this kind of activity very strange and disturbing indeed. But now, after three years of experience and investigation, we've come to accept such odd events as synonymous with the extraordinary phenomena that is the subject of this book.

From the moment the mysterious luminosities first appeared we were enchanted; drawn in by a strange and fascinating enigma.

It is a phenomenon that we have not only been fortunate enough to photograph, but which at times we have also seen and felt, and interacted with.

The events we shall relate began innocuously enough when we photographed our first "orbs". At first we naively thought that orbs were something unique to us but we soon learned that they had been photographed by people all over the world.

However this is not essentially a book about orbs, though at first it may seem so.

As you will see later, our own particular phenomenon evolved from the familiar orbs into something else; quite different and unexpected; something that caused us to question the nature of reality itself.

Suffice it to say here that during the last two and half years we've been amazed, perplexed and inspired by what we've been privileged to experience and photograph. And it was our need to investigate and understand these phenomena that has led us to relate our story. But before we do that; as we are going to be travelling companions on this journey, it may help to briefly introduce ourselves and set the scene for the unfolding of our tale.

My partner Katie is a contemporary artist and I am a designer.

As professional creative people we are used to problem solving and using our critical faculties. Like many we already had an interest in the unknown, and though not scientists or parapsychologists, over the past four years we have had, of necessity, to become researchers and investigators into the paranormal. In that context we have used all the skills and experience available to us to research and investigate the phenomena as rationally as possible; trying to maintain a balance between wonder and scepticism. We naturally have our own personal spiritual perspectives, though like most other ordinary people of reasonable intelligence we've no particular religious bias. Nor do we have any axes to grind; New Age or otherwise.

Though we must point out here, for those with a scientific background, that we realise that this book does not constitute a scientific study, nor do we offer the evidence we have as conclusive proof for the existence of none human intelligences. This is an ordinary person's look at the extraordinary, and in that sense we have sought to do the best we can with the knowledge and evidences available to us.

As to the photographs: initially we were lightening and enhancing images just to see more clearly what exactly was there. Certainly we had no thoughts of reproduction at that time and in that context we must apologise for the loss of detail in some of the images. However, we later learned that it made good sense to save the originals and have tried to strike a balance between best visibility of the luminosities and the over all reproduction quality of the image.

In writing this book we have sought, not only to relate our own personal experience but to also give a more general over-view, in which we cover various viewpoints, even the ones we personally find less credible, as objectively as possible. However it is not possible for us; or for anyone else for that matter, to be truly objective about their own experiences. All personal experience, by its very nature, is subjectively perceived and translated. This is especially true for experiences of extraordinary phenomena. All we can hope for is that the reader may, at the very least, find the subjects of this book as amazing and thought provoking as we do.

Katie and I live in part of a 19th-century house, in middle England, called Brackenbeck. It was once a country mansion with landscaped gardens and woodlands. Sometime in the 1950s it was divided up. But fortunately for us; both gardens and woodland remain much as they were originally; and Brackenbeck still retains an old fashioned appeal that is somehow timeless. Perhaps this is due in part to the diversity of old trees and plants in the gardens or to the energising ions from the rushing stream that winds its way through the grounds. Whatever the reason, Brackenbeck is, to us at least, a special place.

It is within these surroundings that most of our extraordinary experiences with the mysterious luminosities have occurred.

The occurrence of synchronicity (meaningful coincidences) has been integral to this phenomenon on various levels from the beginning, and in the context of the luminosities that have occupied our time and appeared in our photographs, it is interesting to note here that through a chain of "coincidental" events, this book has been published by O Books; and if you look at the publishers raison d'être on their website (www.o-books.net) you will see that this is quite strangely relevant to some of our own thoughts and speculations about circular symbolism.

In symbolic terms, orbs, spheres and circles, have been used throughout history as visual metaphors for infinity, perfection and eternity. They are often a symbol for God and in religious art the circle is the form of the halo. In psychological terms the symmetrical rounded shape of the orb, sphere or circle, represents and encourages feelings of relaxation and inner peace. The Earth itself is a sphere; and within its confines we each follow the circle of our lives. This symbolism is very relevant to our phenomena; and it soon became apparent that what we were photographing had a universality that touched the human psyche.

Wherever we each may be spiritually, and no matter how much we may think we've got it sussed; there is always something; somewhere, waiting to turn our reality upside down and add another mystery to the world we all thought we knew.

In the following pages we offer you an account of our experiences, our unique photographs; and our speculations and insights into strange and mysterious phenomena, which we believe warrants further consideration on many levels.

Hopefully this book may also inspire some readers to explore this phenomenon for themselves. If you already have a digital camera, we would recommend that you check your previous images for possible luminosities; then compare them with the ones we have taken. You may see something new.

If this book sparks your interest in paranormal phenomena, then hopefully you may be inspired to try photographing luminosities for yourself. You may just be in for a surprise – put thought into action and anything can happen!

But be warned. Chasing orbs and other luminosities can be both intriguing and infuriating. As well as a good digital camera, there are three basic attributes any good 'orb hunter' needs in their mental tool kit: a sense of wonder, a sense of reason and, when all else fails; a sense of humour.

May orbs and light-forms be with you!
KATIE HALL & JOHN PICKERING
Brackenbeck, 2006

CHAPTER 1

BEGINNING WITH ORBS

"Spectrum: .a: The complete range of electromagnetic radiation arranged in order of frequency of wavelength.
b: The complete range of colours as dispersed from light."

(READERS DIGEST UNIVERSAL DICTIONARY)

Incredible and inexplicable images! Fantastic mystifying flashes of light! Scintillating spheres! Extraordinary orbs! Luminosities in the lens! All over the world people are photographing something strange. Something that is happening at the speed of light, something which; even as you read this page is happening all around you.

The light that illuminates this page is part of the electromagnetic spectrum, which permeates and surrounds every living thing on our planet. The electromagnetic spectrum ranges from the shortest wavelengths (gamma rays) to the longest (radio waves). The

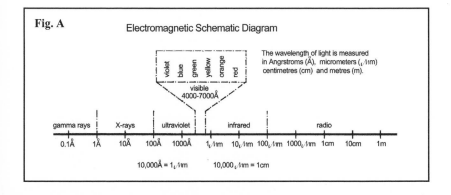

Fig. A   Electromagnetic Schematic Diagram

The wavelength of light is measured in Angrstroms (Å), micrometers (µm) centimetres (cm) and metres (m).

visible
4000-7000Å

violet blue green yellow orange red

gamma rays | X-rays | ultraviolet | infrared | radio

0.1Å   1Å   10Å   100Å   1000Å   1µm   10µm   100µm   1000µm   1cm   10cm   1m

10,000Å = 1µm   10,000 µm = 1cm

wavelength of light is measured in Angstroms, micrometers, centimetres and metres. If we reduce the electromagnetic spectrum to a schematic diagram 157 mm long and mark off sections to represent; gamma rays, X-rays, ultraviolet, infrared and radio waves; the visual spectrum (all that is visible to our eyes) would represent only a mere 5mm on that scale! (Fig. A)

Everything that we can see falls within 4000 – 7000 Angstroms, between ultraviolet and infrared. Though it only represents a small portion of the electromagnetic spectrum, light is indispensable to life. At the biological level it is light that drives photosynthesis in plants, causing life-giving oxygen to be released into our atmosphere. Without light we would not even be here. In Genesis, the first words that God speaks is; 'Let there be light.' And light has been nourishing and sustaining the human soul, physically and spiritually ever since. Light is universally seen as a symbol of spiritual enlightenment. In Judaism, Christianity and Islam, in particular, light is often used as a metaphor, for God, truth, virtue and spirituality. Light shines out in many forms throughout the world; the light of life; the light of love; the light of reason; and though the lamps be many, light is one and all. For the photographer and artist; light is both the inspiration and the means of expression.

It was as leisurely strolling amateur photographers that we first encountered the extraordinary light phenomenon that is the subject of this book. Drawn in by the fascinating enigma of the mysterious luminosities, we soon found ourselves on a journey into the unknown.

As with most journeys it began in familiar territory. It happened the day we took our first photograph of an orb. But first things first. What is an orb?

For those not familiar with the term, and to whom an 'orb' may be something that is part of the monarch's ceremonial regalia, it is worth mentioning here that orbs, like ball lightning and earth lights, fall into the rather controversial area of anomalous light phenomena. Some would more definitively say; paranormal phenomena.

For a few years now, people all over the world have been photographing strange spheres, disks and balls of light, a phenomenon commonly known as orbs.

None of this was known to us three years ago, when we took our first photograph of an orb, though for hundreds of years people have reported seeing strange and mysterious lights of all kinds. Since the invention of photography there have been many occurrences of odd anomalous lights that have appeared on prints and negatives. Some of these rather puzzling images were subsequently found to be natural light effects or even, hoaxes, but many of them just could not be explained in ordinary terms.

For those who consider these genuine photographic anomalies to be evidence of paranormal phenomena, they are usually categorised as either orbs, vapours, vortices or apparitions. Orbs in particular have recently been photographed by people all over the world, with all types of cameras, but they occur most frequently in digital images.

To avoid confusion over terminology, and for the purposes of this book, we will use the terms orbs, vortices and spheres as being synonymous with what we have collectively defined as 'luminosities'. And although we shall still at times use all four descriptive terms in certain contexts, we have our reasons for considering them all to be essentially the same phenomenon, as will become clear. Orbs are the most widely recurring form of photographable luminosities, but it is interesting to note that since the development and proliferation of digital cameras, the occurrence of spheres, disks and other orb-like photographic anomalies has increased rather than decreased. This seems rather odd as one would have thought that with more technologically sophisticated cameras, the reverse would be true. But the fact is the majority of orbs are captured on digital cameras and camcorders.

Discounting the possibility of a worldwide outbreak of the same digital processing malfunction in every make of camera, causing the same effects across a whole variety of conditions, it would be reasonable to concede the possibility that the images of orbs taken by a wide variety of people may indeed be a real phenomena worth investigating with an open mind.

Naturally, these images have attracted both interest and criticism. Like Crop Circles, orbs have their convinced believers and entrenched sceptics. Realistically a percentage of orb-like effects will undoubtedly be due to lens flare or flash feedback. However, any one seriously interested in this phenomenon should not be put off by debunkers glibly trotting out these explanations as conclusive. This is definitely far from the facts, as we have discovered.

In January 2002, our first digital camera, a Umax 800 pixel, had finally packed up. We'd had the Umax for two years and though we'd had a lot of fun with it

We had never, in all that time, taken anything resembling an orb or any other kind of luminosities or light effects that are the focus of this book. At that time we had no experience of or interest in orbs. But we now had to look around for another camera and bought an Olympus C200 with 2.1 Megapixels and 3 times optical zoom.

We were soon thoroughly enjoying our new toy and used the camera regularly: including taking reference shots for Katie's paintings, as well as all the usual snapshots. By the end of March we had easily taken over 300 shots in all kinds of lighting conditions, indoors and outdoors. In the context of what follows we must emphasise here that again at no time then did we get orbs, or any other kind of luminosities on any of our photographs at all. This is worth bearing in mind, because all that soon changed.

One sunny afternoon at the beginning of April 2002, we were out walking through an avenue of old woodland trees that lined a nearby riverside walk. We took a few photos of one or two of the most interesting trees for reference (Picture 1). When we enlarged our images we noticed that one of the shots had an odd kind of coloured light effect on it. Floating about a third of the way up the trunk of a large tree was what looked like a ball of blue and pink light. It certainly hadn't been visible in the viewfinder when Katie took the photo.

The odd light ball appeared to be transparent, its colours similar to a gas fire flame, its structure resembling a plasma globe, about the size of a ten-pin bowling ball. In addition there was a second smaller white light below it. We wondered if these effects may be light bouncing off the lens somehow?

We had both used SLR cameras a fair bit and knew about lens flare, but this explanation seemed unlikely as the sunlight hadn't been glaringly bright along the path. Probably we would have simply written off this odd image as a photo anomaly and left it at that, had it not been for a second similar occurrence the very next weekend.

The following Friday night, after dinner, I took a couple of shots of Katie, by the fireside, in a new pink dress that she had recently purchased. During that week we had taken quite a few shots, with flash

and without flash. There had not been a single 'light ball' on any of them. So we never gave it a further thought, not until the Saturday morning, when we looked at the photos from the night before. There on the carpet just in front of Katie was an odd little ball of light.

We were both instantly reminded of the light ball in the tree. Except that this, unlike the one in the tree, was small and mostly white. Could they be the same thing? Was our new camera on the blink? Now spurred on by curiosity we took more shots in the front room just to see if we'd get the same kind of light ball effect again. And much to our surprise we did, though at the time we saw nothing at all until we uploaded the images to the computer. The strange light balls were apparently not visible to the human eye. At least not at first. During the weeks that followed we found that on roughly a quarter of our shots we were now getting light balls, or spheres, as we began to call them.

This was very interesting but also very puzzling, because although we took lots of shots elsewhere in and around the house, we only got "spheres" in the front room! This seemed very odd. And, as time went on we also noticed that orbs seemed to appear more frequently when people were around. One of the later shots (photo 3) shows Sam and accompanying orbs. See if you can spot a critical factor on this photograph. We'll come back to it later in Chapter 5.

There didn't seem to be any pattern to their appearance; sometimes the spheres were there, sometimes they weren't; nor did there seem to be any obvious technologi-cal reason for them to be on some shots and not on others. Shots that in many instances had been taken using the same camera settings in the same place with the same lighting conditions - it was all rather mystifying!

Was this something unique to us or was it something to do with the house? After a couple of months, we had accumulated quite a lot of images with odd little light balls on them but still had no real explanation as to what they were or why they were there.

After some deliberation we decided to show some of our light sphere photographs to a good friend who we trusted, and who had once been a professional photographer. Dave studied the images on the computer screen in silence. We waited apprehensively, both half expecting him to say, "Get a new camera!", but he didn't. Taking another sip of his Earl Grey, he said "These look like orbs to me."

Katie and I looked at each other. Orbs?

Though the term seemed vaguely familiar, we had no real idea at that point what orbs were. But they sounded interesting. We asked him to tell us more. As Dave explained all about the orbs phenomena we realised that these odd balls of light were not unique to us after all. People all over the world were photographing orbs. There was even a proliferation of websites for people who were interested in the subject. This made us feel pretty out of touch. We had been so busy photographing our own phenomena, we'd not even thought of checking on the internet. This certainly proved the old adage that "there's nothing new under the sun". It also seemed to indicate that right in front of our digital lens something strange was going on. But what exactly was it? We were now determined to try and understand what we were photographing, and started to gather as much information as we could on orbs and any other related phenomena. Some weeks later we had been through most of the websites and had a pretty good idea of the whole phenomena in general, though admittedly explanations seemed fairly thin on the ground.

Mysteriously our own orbs, as we were now calling them in common with everyone else, stubbornly continued to only appear in one room! This wasn't right.

We'd already considered the usual possible causes, such as moisture, dust, lens flare or flash feedback. But realistically none of these accounted for what we were photographing. At that time we were just learning about the phenomena – on our feet, so to speak – and each week seemed to give us something else to think about. We didn't realise it then but we were getting hooked!

Neither of us have any bias towards any one spiritual path; like most people, we use the experience and the knowledge we've accumulated to measure the truth about most things. Neither of us align ourselves with any religion or New Age movement, though we do believe that many branches of spiritual experience, once shared common roots. We have, I hope, a fairly unbiased approach to philosophical and spiritual issues. Over the past few years I'd been vaguely aware of a new upsurge of interest in the paranormal. Sceptics had largely written this off as due to all the hype surrounding the advent of the New Millennium. But the fact is, many people, probably more than we realise, experience what are, in terms of normal every-day life, very extraordinary events. A large percentage of this, as we later discovered, is strange phenomenon in the visual spectrum, an area which includes orbs and other forms of luminosities, such as Ghost-lights and UFOs.

Some people, whilst accepting that strange, inexplicable phenomena occur – just don't want to question it any further. And a few are disturbed by even the suggestion that reality may be different to what they're familiar with. They just don't want to know about it at all. Possibly because it may threaten what they already believe. Then of course, some folks are just natural born sceptics, not prone to believe anything they have not physically seen or experienced themselves. And then, there are those who, for various reasons, actually deny what they know to be true.

However, for some people the fact that extraordinary anomalies and paranormal events occur at all, is itself a clue that the ordinary everyday world we all take for granted is not all there is. There is much more to discover.

And so it was for us; but the appearance of orbs was only just the beginning of our journey of discovery!

Critical Angles:*
Question: Does the fact that the orbs phenomena is photographed worldwide, by a variety of people using a wide variety of cameras indicate that this phenomena is not generated by local conditions or

peculiar to any make of camera?

Answer: Yes.

Question: Can the fact that over a period of time we had only been able to photograph orbs in one specific room but nowhere else in the house, be explained adequately in terms of a digital camera malfunction?

Answer: No.

*Critical angle: the smallest angle of incidence at which a light ray passing from one medium to another less refractive medium can be totally reflected from the boundary between the two.

CHAPTER 2

THE APPEARANCE OF
A PHENOMENON

"Luminosity: The condition or quality of being luminous...
The attribute of an object or colour that enables the
observation of the extent to which an object emits light."

(READERS DIGEST UNIVERSAL DICTIONARY)

Only as a flower is man honoured upon earth...
My song unfolds her petals: behold these myriad flowers:

ANCIENT AZTEC SONG.

By 2003 it was obvious that, whatever they were, we definitely had
orbs in residence at Brackenbeck, but in the wider world beyond our
little haven, the world we all knew was changing, on many levels and
in many instances not for the better.

New Millennium politicians now seemed more like managers
working to commercial incentives, rather than caring leaders working
for the good of humanity. The gap between the rich and poor was
widening. An increasing daily diet of media "junk food" was pouring
out of television stations - and even the most conservative of thinking
people had begun to suspect that the dumbing down of society was at
last really happening.

In amongst all the pro-acquisitive hype; the plethora of fatuous
reality TV celebrities and the seemingly endless production of new

generations of hi-tech consumables, many sensed a spiritual void at the very core of our culture. The crumbling of moral and social foundations diverted from public attention by political hype and spin. Which like a band aid over an ulcer, merely concealed the fact that no one was actually dealing with the real problem. But most people were too busy to think about it too much. It has been said that the behaviour of any society depends on its collective view of itself. No matter what their protestations over the media, both Western and Eastern leaders seemed to exhibit the same kind of aggressive defensiveness, which comes from fear of the unknown; or perhaps from fear of what they knew of themselves? Either way decisions made out of fear never lead to security.

Fortunately at Brackenbeck we were not directly affected by all the political double talk spinning in the airwaves; nor by the diabolical activities of terrorist fanatics. Though we only need to look at history to see that lunacy is the natural consequence of fundamentalism of any persuasion.

Amidst the general feeling of fear and uncertainty at that time, we, in our small corner of the world, for some unknown reason, had a positive feeling of expectancy, as though waiting for something good - though we had no idea what it was.

We continued to happily and consistently photograph orbs, though, still very puzzlingly; nowhere else in the house or garden, except for our front room!

Typical of the shots we took at that time is one that shows me apparently looking up at three orbs by the light fitting. I wish I could say this is what actually happened, but, it's an illusion, in fact I saw no orbs at that time. They only showed up on the digital image.

When we first started photographing orbs we usually got only one or two in a single shot so we were quite pleased whenever we managed to get a few on the same image. One evening Katie took a shot of Bugs and Sylvester on one of the settees; to send to the kids. A small group of orbs had decided to drop in to be photographed too.

As we mentioned, orbs are the most often photographed form of what paranormal investigators consider to be four basic photographic manifestations of psychic phenomenon, the other three being vortices, vapours and apparitions. Orbs usually appear lighter than the background photograph and come in a variety of colours. Many showing a faceted disk-like structure, some whitish spheres with blue or pink tints. We've also occasionally had bright orange coloured orbs.

At this point in time we were getting well known amongst close relatives and friends for our rather strange past time of orb photography. One weekend we had Katie's brother Sam staying with us and we invited my daughter and son-in-law over for a meal. After dinner the conversation turned to orbs and we showed them some of our latest photographs. Annabel was keen for us to take some shots that evening. Sam and George, our son-in-law, a computer analyst, and, like Sam, a complete sceptic as far as the paranormal went, proposed an experiment. George had brought his own brand new Canon digital camera with him. The idea being for us to each take shots in the front room and see what happened.

The proviso being that we must first remove any obvious reflective objects, such as the mirror over the fire place; which George and Sam believed to be a probable cause of the phenomena.

As George was the one with the most scientific approach, we let him take charge of the proceedings. Of course we had no idea whether or not we would get any orbs at all. Like cats they were wont to do their own thing and liable to disappear off somewhere else, just when you needed them to stay put. Anyway, we dutifully removed all the obvious causes of reflections to George and Sam's satisfaction. The room was now ready to put the orbs, and us, to the test.

We now each randomly took a few shots, with both cameras, Katie with our Olympus and George with his Canon. We uploaded the ones from the Olympus to the computer, but couldn't do the same with the Canon shots, because, unknown to George, until then, our USB lead for the Olympus wasn't compatible with his camera. Stone Age technology was mentioned; the Olympus being two years older than the Canon, but we nobly ignored that. Two years in digital camera terms seems to equate to about 200 years anywhere else.

But we were able to check the Canon shots on the camera screen. Neither of had got anything! To George and Sam, at least, this seemed to validate their mirror theory. However, we hoped we knew better, orbs being the elusive things they are. Off we went for another try; this time George and I taking the pictures. Then, on the sixth shot on our Olympus there they were.

The photo showed Katie and about eight orbs. Mostly we only got one or two in the front room, so we were both very pleased by this. George and Sam, however, weren't quite so pleased, as this blew the mirror theory. Not wanting to concede a point, in a slightly mock grumbling tone, Sam said; "OK, then. But I'd be more impressed if you'd got a whole roomful."

As there were no orbs on the rest of the shots, we all trooped back into the front room for another go. George and Sam's scepticism was now diluted but still, half jokingly, present. The mood was light and humorous. In fact we were all probably getting a bit silly by then. We took a few more random snaps with both the Olympus and the Canon. And this time even

George got a couple, but when we clicked through our Olympus images everyone was instantly silenced. This photograph showed a whole room full of orbs. It was amazing!

(Photo.7.) The number of orbs on this photograph borders on the incredible, especially taking into account Sam's previous comment, about him being more impressed if we'd got a whole roomful. And that was exactly what happened!

It was just as if the orbs were making a definite statement! Katie, Sam and Bel all got goose-bumps and George could hardly believe his eyes. This had never happened before and it has never happened since. The luminosities seemed to have responded directly to Sam. He was visibly staggered. Their timing was perfect.

The appearance of a roomful of orbs at that precise time amazed everyone.

But typical of our elusive luminosities, on the very next image there were only a meagre three orbs, and none on any of the other images. Nor on any of the photographs we shot later that evening with either the Olympus or the Canon.

They seemed to have made their point and gone. However, to placate George's dwindling scepticism, we later tried, and failed, to purposefully recreate the effect. Using both cameras we did double flash shots, both with the light on and with it off. In desperation George and Sam even put the mirror back and tried to bounce flash reflections off that, without any result that looked anything like an orb. The experiment had proved one thing: it had been impossible for us to create even one genuine looking orb effect using mirror reflections, let alone a whole roomful! But it certainly gave us all cause for thought. What happened that night was either an incredible coincidence or it suggested some kind of deliberate interaction at work, specifically directed at the people in that room at that time. If the latter: then the luminosities had responded dramatically and unequivocally. Sam and George had a lot to think about and we, of course, were delighted. As far as we know no one else has ever photographed so many orbs inside one room on a single shot. The final count was over two hundred!

Taken on its own what exactly happened here is, of course, open to question.

But in terms of our phenomena in general this proved not to be an isolated incidence of purposeful response by the luminosities. In that context it suggested that our mysterious luminosities had the facility to initiate responses. And if that was true the phenomena seemed able to demonstrate other qualities that went far beyond static two-dimensional digital images.

Critical Angles:

Question: Does the appearance of orbs on photographs in a room where major reflective surfaces have been removed suggest that orbs are the result of some other process than reflection?

Answer: Yes.

Question: Does the appearance of orbs specifically relative to, and seemingly in response to, a verbal observation suggest the possibility that orbs may be something other than two-dimensional images?

Answer: Yes!

CHAPTER 3

LUMINOSITIES IN THE GARDEN

And God said, let there be Light and there was Light. And God saw the Light that it was good: and God divided the Light from the Darkness.

GENESIS. 1.3 & 4.

The known is finite, the unknown infinite: intellectually we stand on an islet in the midst of an illimitable ocean of inexplicability. Our business in every generation is to reclaim a little more land.

T.H. HUXLEY, 1887

By the end of 2003 we had accumulated stacks of images of orbs, all taken in our front room, but so far we had completely failed to get them to show up anywhere else. Early in 2004 the weather took a drastic turn for the worse. Rain came down in antediluvian quantities. The local river burst its banks and the nearby town was cut off for over a day. Fortunately we are situated several miles away and Brackenbeck stands on high ground. Even so, the stream that ran through the garden flooded. Water poured down the drive and the cats came scurrying indoors.

The day after the deluge was a Tuesday in February and though the ground was sodden and soggy the afternoon was dry. Two adults and three cats trooped out into the garden with the intention of photographing the swollen stream and any thing else that may be photographically interesting. After a lot of squelching about through the undergrowth we took a few photographs of the stream in full flood. When we uploaded the images we were surprised

and excited by what we saw. For the first time we had a photograph of orbs in the garden. It showed two orbs flying over the flooded stream in daylight.

But although we'd taken five or six shots (all without flash) we only had orbs on one photograph. Even though the lighting and the camera settings were the same, all the other shots were orb free as had been the norm up till then.

But getting even just one image prompted us to try our luck again and indeed thereafter we got more orbs on the photographs we took in the garden. Not all the time, but often enough to be statistically interesting, in view of the fact that previously we had taken lots of shots in the grounds and not got anything at all. What had made the difference? We had no instant answers. But it was thought provoking. The only common denominator seemed to be the sudden appearance of the two orbs over the stream, just as in the beginning when we'd been taking photographs indoors but not getting any orbs until the first one appeared on the carpet in front of Katie. Was there a correlation here? It seemed a bit coincidental. But we didn't think much more of it at that time.

Spring was well on the way and we were soon photographing orbs

throughout the whole of the garden. It was an intriguing pastime, which especially fascinated Katie. In the evening, more often than not, we would go out together to try our luck. Usually we were accompanied by the cats, who perhaps wondered why the humans were now traipsing about through the woods most evenings. And we must admit that at first it was something of a novelty and orb-hunting become our favourite evening pastime. We got orbs in the shrubbery. (Photo. 9.)

And over the stream. (Photo. 10.)

And amongst the trees in the woodland. (Photo. 11.)

Even though we were now photographing orbs all over the garden, their appearances tended to be fairly intermittent but the one place where we got them consistently was in a little dell next to the stream. In this secluded corner a small ash tree stands in a circle of old-fashioned plants including, alkanet and lungwort, commonly called 'Soldiers and Sailors' because of its red and blue flowers. Lungwort was used to cure bronchial diseases by herbalists in past times. It had obviously been deliberately planted long ago, and in March the whole circle is covered in bright yellow daffodils. Katie had

always called this place the 'Faerie Dell', even before the orbs appeared. And she had always felt it to be a special place. The fact that we could usually photograph orbs around there if we hadn't found them anywhere else in the garden, seemed to bear this out. (Photo. 12.)

One evening, together with the cats, we were out trying our luck, when Katie noticed our oldest cat, Thomas, paying particular attention to something not visible to us. Going with her instincts she quickly took a shot. The resulting photograph showed both a cat and an orb. (Photo. 13.)

Could this have been what had attracted Thomas's attention?

Thomas passed peacefully away at the ripe old age of 18, while we were writing this book. But thanks to Thomas, we got our first photograph of a luminosity and a cat together. This made us wonder if cats, according to their reputation, really had a sixth sense. And if they did; could they see orbs, or sense whatever causes them? Thomas always seemed to be unnervingly seeing things that weren't there.

But knowing Thomas, that was probably just for effect, to keep the humans on their toes. After all, cats do have a mysterious reputation to live up to.

Even so, Katie did well to get the shot of Thomas and orb. Because cats, like children, unless they are asleep, have usually moved by the time you've pressed shutter release. And photographing cats outside at night can often result in orbs of a different kind. Cats' eyes all too easily reflect flash and we would sometimes find, not orbs, but two big saucer-like searchlights staring back at us from the image.

Fortunately that didn't happen on this next occasion, when a couple of weeks later, Katie got a shot of me and Oscar, our ginger cat, and orbs in the background. (Photo. 14.)

But our best cat shot so far, was taken a few months later. (Photo. 15.)

In this instance Oscar almost seemed to be reacting up to the

luminosities as if he knew, or sensed, they were there. Unfortunately though, the cats didn't seem predisposed to share what they may or may not know about orbs with us mere humans, so we had to struggle on trying to make sense of it on our own.

Some nights the orbs seemed to be everywhere outside, then for no apparent reason the elusive luminosities would simply disappear and that was the end of the photo session. Some nights we'd get nothing at all, not even in the Faerie Dell. In terms of any natural, and certainly any technological, explanations for what was happening this didn't make any sense whatsoever.

But as we got more experienced in our outside orb-hunting we began to amass an archive of photographs taken with the Olympus. We were happy with the images we were getting, but as a photographer friend pointed out, when it came to verifying our results we should at least also be using one other make of camera, to rule out totally that the orbs we were photographing were not restricted to shots taken by the Olympus. And so we decided to look for a new middle-range camera that was likely to be typical of the kind of thing most people would buy and use. Eventually we bought a Pentax Optio 30 with 3.2 Megapixels and a 5.8mm lens with 3 times optical zoom capability. We then used both cameras when trying to photograph orbs. Though in this book black and white has been used, our original photographs are in colour.

These and others can be seen on our website at: www.lights2beyond.com

A BIT ABOUT PHOTOGRAPHING ORBS
We must point out here that we never used the digital zoom facility on either camera because digital zoom tends to degrade the image too

much, and we wanted to get the best shots we could. Naturally those taken outdoors at night vary anyway, according to lighting conditions. Some are obviously better than others. If the conditions were very dark we found we had to lighten up those images quite considerably on the computer in order to see exactly what we had got – but in general we tried to shoot at dusk, when there was still a little light.

Ideally the night has to be dark enough to see the luminosities but not so dark that you have to lighten up the photographs too much and lose detail. As a general rule, we also avoid taking shots in the rain, or in humid or misty conditions, as this could lead to the possibility of water droplets reflecting in the flash and giving an orb-like effect. Though if you compare images taken in the wet with genuine orbs taken in dry conditions, there is a definite difference. However, it is advisable, when trying to photograph orbs outside, to choose conditions that minimise the possibility of any weather or atmospheric related effects. Our advice to anyone embarking on this pursuit would be to frequent places where orbs have already consistently occurred,

as they seem to have favourite spots, but to keep trying new locations as well.

We were now largely preoccupied with outdoor photography, and had more or less abandoned taking indoor shots. It is worth mentioning here that since photographing orbs in the garden we were now also getting them in the rest of the house as well, not just in one room as before. As far as our outdoor shots went, there seemed to be no particular pattern that we could detect to the occurrence of orbs. Except, just as with the living room shots; they seemed to occur more frequently in proximity to people. I would often photograph them near to Katie. (Photo. 16.)

And around, or near to, visiting friends. (Photo. 17.)

As we mentioned earlier, though we took photographs in the garden at different times of day, we generally tended to favour dusk and early dark shots. And at these times we would sometimes also get luminosities floating around the front of Brackenbeck . (Photo. 18.)

If you look closely you'll see that near the house are also one or two odd shapes in the sky. What they are we don't know. One friend thought he could discern a grey alien-like face, but in this case we're more inclined to believe this is due to our human tendency for making recognisable images out of random patterns. Not that we have anything against the Alien hypothesis in general. But aliens are sometimes trotted out as an all too convenient answer for all kinds of strange phenomena. It's a bit like saying God did it! That is not to say that

aliens don't exist or, if they do, don't interact with terrestrial humans. But that is another matter and there are plenty of books worth reading for those interested in the subject.

The more we looked for answers to the orbs, the more we felt that we should try and view the phenomena in a more holistic context, rather than just automatically sticking it into the ghosts or aliens slot. For a start we had to take into consideration the fact that something which can be photographed at all is, for a time, no matter how briefly, present in the visual spectrum. And everything that appears in the visual spectrum has to conform to known physical laws just to be there. It seemed reasonable therefore to assume that the fact the luminosities were a photographable phenomena must tell us something about their nature. Perhaps this would give us a clue as to what they really were?

Critical Angles:

Question: Does the sudden appearance of orbs and luminosities in the garden, where before it had proved impossible to photgraph them in any conditions, suggest that the phenomena is responding to some factor, other than weather or technology?

Answer: Yes.

Question: If it is possible, as their behaviour indicates, for cats to see luminosities, does this suggest that the phenomena may be present in the visual spectrum at some detectable frequency?

Answer: Yes.

CHAPTER 4

LIGHT AND ILLUMINATION

"Light: n. electromagnetic radiation by which things are visible."

(COLLINS POCKET ENGLISH DICTIONARY)

I have set my rainbow in the clouds, and it shall be a sign...

GENESIS. 9.13.

There was a young lady named Bright,
Who travelled much faster than light.
She started one day
In a relative way
And returned on the previous night.

ARTHUR BULLER.

As this book is chiefly concerned with unusual light phenomena, in this chapter we shall look further into the nature of light: what it is and how it works.

When a ray of sunlight travels through a raindrop it is split into all the colours of the rainbow. Rainbows have been used as symbols of luck, fortune and happiness throughout history. It was the rainbow that inspired Isaac Newton's work on light.

Though Newton is best known for his law of gravity which was set out in the Principia in 1687, his other great scientific work was the

Optics, published in 1704 and based on the experiments he made as a young man to discover the nature of light.

Newton's experiments with prisms led him to the discovery that white light is in reality made up of a variety of coloured rays, in fact, all the colours seen in the rainbow. Newton's idea that white light was not after all, pure, met with forceful derisory opposition, especially from the Romantic poets, who later condemned Newton for removing mystery from the universe; claiming that he had destroyed the beauty of the rainbow by his prism and reduced the world to mere fact and reason.

Although Newton himself, in his Optics, pointed out that colour itself is mysterious.

Why certain objects reflect particular rays of colour and how those rays effect the eye's ability to perceive those colours was inexplicable to Newton. But in1803 the English physicist, Thomas Young, finally proved that light behaved like a wave, not like a particle. Young's simple but conclusive demonstration of this changed the way scientists viewed the nature of light. Then much later along came, Albert Einstein with the idea that light contained photons. This conflicted with Young's wave theory of light. Even to this day the argument is on going as to whether light is made up of photonic particles or waves. Paradoxically light can be viewed as either, depending on the conditions.

In attempting to explain this problem, over the years, scientists have come up with some odd ideas, such as Einstein's notion that photons may be guided by what he termed: "ghost waves" or the quantum physicists' mathematical loophole idea of: "probability waves". But it seems unlikely that science will be able to fully answer the paradox of light, until scientists understand the full nature of gravity, electricity, and magnetism. Are they primary forces in themselves, or by-products of fundamental forces still undiscovered? As yet, no one really knows.

The scientists' problem in defining the nature and behaviour of light was best described by Werner Heisenberg, the 20th-century German physicist, who recognised the tremendous conceptual problems faced by physicists whose research forced them to think in totally new categories about the nature of reality, which he described as, "something standing in the middle between the idea of an event and the actual event..." His work led to the formulation of what is known as the Heisenberg uncertainty principle. It consists of a set of mathematical relations that determine the limits by which classical concepts may be applied to atomic phenomena. In effect defining the limits of human imagination in the subatomic world, where scientists can no longer be detached, objective, observers, because they are actually involved in the world which they observe.

In the atomic world scientists influence the properties of observed objects, simply by the act of observing and measuring them. If you think this has somewhat mystical overtones, you would be right. The universe described by modern atomic physics is a dynamic inseparable whole, in which the observer is always essentially included. In this reality, the classical concepts of space and time, of cause and effect and of isolated objects totally lose their meaning. This is especially true in the realm of quantum physics in which scientific theories often run parallel to reality as described by Eastern mysticism.

In spite of years of mind-stretching theories and brain-boggling concepts, it wasn't until 1963 that scientists were able to define the mechanism by which our eyes and brain are able to recognise colours. Inadequate theories had been bandied about since Newton's time, until the year, that the same defining discovery was made, practically simultaneously, by several scientists in different parts of the world. It was one of those strange synchronistic events (and we shall look more closely at synchronicity in Chapter 13), that has happened before in the history of progress; almost as if the time was right for a particular discovery.

Essentially it boils down to this: in the human eye there are three different types of colour vision cells, each with a different visual pigment. These cells, called cones, each respond to a different section of the colour spectrum.

Cone A: deep blue-violet = wavelength of 450 manometers.
Cone B: dark green = wavelength of 525 manometers.
Cone C: dark yellow = wavelength of 555 manometers.

Surprisingly this natural selection of colour cones contradicted previous assumptions that all colour receptors in the eye would be made up from the same basic colour set as we use in colour television: red, green and blue. Instead, nature chose a combination from which all other colours can be derived.

But no one is sure exactly why, out of the whole electromagnetic spectrum, nature chose 4000 – 7000 Angstroms, between ultraviolet and infrared, to sense colour movement and form. Perhaps this is because higher frequencies give better definition? Although ultra-violet light has a higher frequency than visible light and in micro-technology, in particular, it often gives better definition than visible light but in the higher bandwidths it is fairly dangerous to our well being.

When God said 'Let there be light!' he introduced a fundamental physical and spiritual principle that affects our lives on practically every level. When light enters the eye about 20% of it travels past the retina to reach the brain. Here it affects such vital components as the pituitary gland, the hypothalamus and the pineal gland. It is possible that visible light, and quite probably the rest of the electromagnetic spectrum, affects most of our vital life processes. Recent evidence suggests that it does indeed affect such processes as hormone production, the autonomic nervous system and stress responses – it may even have the power to alter our metabolic rate and reproductive functions.

Light from the sun not only enriches our experience of life and gives us warmth, it helps us to metabolise vitamin D, without which we would be calcium deficient, and sunlight itself is a powerful bactericide. Many frequencies of the electromagnetic spectrum are now commonly used by us for manufacture, communication and healing. Infra-red, which can be transmitted through objects that block visible light, is not only used for night vision and wireless communication, it has a beneficial effect on skin and tissue. Polarised light can boost the immune system, X-rays can detect injuries, ultra-violet light is used to irradiate tissue and cleanse blood. SADS (Seasonally Affected Disorder Syndrome) is caused by lack of natural light and full spectrum light has been used to treat this with positive results. Even NASA use full spectrum lighting in their spacecraft.

Indian Yogis believe that the body contains Chakras, seven spinning discs of coloured lights, which interestingly are the same colours as the spectrum. This seems to support the theory that colour affects our feelings and actions. And perhaps it should not be surprising that both science and mysticism compliment each other in the view that our bodies are responsive to the energy fields that make up and surround us. In recent times the idea that we as living beings, resonate with the colour spectrum and are affected by various colours has been used with positive results by colour therapists.

Some people even claim to be able to actually see auras: the invisible fields of etheric, astral, mental and causal energy, which surround the human body. Though the descriptions of this vary, depending on either a scientific or spiritual perspective, there is now little doubt that all organic beings radiate energy fields.

If, for example: you pointed a radio telescope at an isolated person, it would pick up radio emissions from that individual, in much the same manner as it would from a distant star. Latent heat cameras can be used to view heat impressions of people long after they've left a room. Those who can see auras are often able to use this ability to diagnose various illnesses, though in the main the idea of auras is still frowned on by orthodox medicine, it is worth bearing in mind that once in the not too distant past, anything other than bleeding, or using leeches, was also frowned upon by the learned doctors of the time.

Interestingly scientific research has recently appeared to confirm the ancient assertions of Yogis and mystics that our body is made up of light. They have made the discovery that all living organisms, from animal tissue cells to the cells of trees and plants, have the facility to collect and emit light. In effect this means that your body acts like a transceiver, picking up and sending out rays of light all the time. And although these light rays cannot be seen with the naked eye, they have now been measured by a number of researchers throughout the world and are known as Bio-photons.

The frequency of Bio-photons is very weak, but also very important. Bio-photons are stored in skin cells and within DNA molecules. They go right to the core of our being. At the International

Institute of Biophysics in Germany, scientists have shown that Bio-photons are a ubiquitous phenomenon of all organic systems. This has been confirmed by other researchers in Japan and Russia. Interestingly, it seems that diseased cells, such as cancer cells, do not have the ability to store Bio-photons and the indications are that they can even be damaged by them. So, ancient Eastern teachings about us being "containers of light"; or old Oriental spiritual exercises for "drawing in the light"; or the Biblical view of "living in the light"; may all have actual parallels in the world of physics!

Isn't it amazing how so much that has been previously derided by sceptics, experts and scientists as delusional or unscientific, simply because it came from a mystical or spiritual perspective; has been later shown to be true. But perhaps the nature of orthodoxy throughout history and in all areas of our society is to try and convince us that it alone has the answers, when sometimes it doesn't even understand the questions.

Murray Cohen once said: "The ark was built by amateurs, and the Titanic by experts. Don't wait for the experts."

A brief reflection on what you may have personally experienced in your own dealings with those in authority, in management, and in any form of orthodox practices whether medical, educational or scientific may well verify the truth of this remark. And light, as we have seen in our brief photon-driven tour around the subject, is itself by no means a cut and dried subject. Even in our knowledge of light there are still the shadows of mystery. We still do not know definitively how we are able to visually perceive the world around us. The exact nature of light is still unresolved: whether it is a wave, a particle or both, is still open for discussion. Recently there is even controversy in scientific circles about the actual speed of light: one of the critical constants physicists and astronomers need to make Einstein's relative universe absolute.

In schools it has always been taught as an absolute fact that light travels at a constant speed of 300,000 kilometres per second. Everywhere, all the time!

The speed of light has been taught as a universal constant. But it now seems that the speed of light may not after all be constant. It has changed. The leading exponent of this is Australian scientist Barry Setterfield, who collated measurements made by sixteen different methods over 300 years. These measurements show that the speed of light has decreased from the first recorded observation until it levelled off around 1960. And even more controversially, recent deep space observations indicate that some distant objects are actually moving faster than the speed of light. These objects are called, "superluminals" and have been observed as moving many times faster than the currently accepted speed of light. So what does this mean? Well, if the speed of light is not actually constant; and only appears to be constant in certain circumstances; this will have devastating consequences for astronomy and cosmology. For it is upon the supposition that the speed of light is constant at 300,000 kilometres per second that all interstellar distances are measured. Astronomers measure distance in terms of parsecs, more commonly known as light years. (A light year is simply the distance travelled by a ray of light in one year.) This measurement is based solely on the fact that light always travels at 300,000 kilometres per second, and so a light year roughly works out at ten million, million kilometres.

But surely a few light years here or there is not a real problem – or is it?

Yes, it is! If the speed of light is not constant at 300,000 kilometres per second then that radically affects the distance, and age of astronomical objects. This in turn affects our view of the age of the universe, our solar system; and subsequently, the whole concept of the expanding universe, upon which our present cosmology is based. Oops! What was it Murray Cohen said? Are we seeing the light yet?

At one time in medieval Europe "experts" of the day were busily discussing how many angels could fit on a pin head – today, their 21st-century counterparts are discussing, with a lot more knowledge, of course, how the whole universe came into being out of a single explosion; called the Big Bang. This accidental cosmic explosion of something, before there was anything, (according to the theory) caused an immense flash of light, which generated all the energy and matter that makes up the universe today. You, me; everything there is; began somewhere between 10,000 million and 20,000 million years ago – we know this (again according to the theory) because the residual heat from the primeval inferno of the explosion can be measured because the speed of light is a universal constant at 300,000 kilometres per second!

But then again – perhaps this is not what happened at all?

As Katie and I looked at the nature of light and what it may mean, not only for our own understanding of our luminosities in particular; but for a wider understanding of the universe around us; we felt, like amateur investigators the world over, a sense of excitement at the growing realisation that perhaps, just perhaps, we were on to something. Light, by which we saw and photographed our phenomena; was in its self both wonderful and mysterious; part of us all in ways only previously described by ancient mystics. And all the evidence suggested that Light had a spiritual, as well as a physical effect on humanity.

In our small corner of the cosmos, as we bombarded another luminosity with photon emissions from the camera flash; causing it to imprint as a digital image, we had a lot to think about. Looking at these images had caused us to look more closely at light itself. And as we reflected on our strange phenomena, we were struck by the thought that all photography, whatever the subject matter, is essentially about photographing light. Photographically it is both the means and the end. And if our bodies really are transceivers of light, collecting and radiating electromagnetic energy and Bio-photons, then both the photographer and the subject are connected at some level by a dynamic process. Both small elements caught up perhaps in a universal dance of light!

Critical Angles:

Question: If science is unable to precisely define what gravity, electricity and magnetism actually are, is it able to define the nature of light beyond all doubt?

Answer: No.

CHAPTER 5

NEGATIVE ANSWERS AND PUZZLING PIXELS

"Experiments have acquainted us with a paradoxical fact: man can see "correctly" only because of his imagination. The human eye, optically speaking, is a piece of bad workmanship ...yet man ...does not notice anything ...the nervous system corrects these faults so perfectly that we perceive a technically flawless image of our surroundings."

The Magic of The Senses, VITUS B. DROSCHER.

As we accumulated more images of the luminosities at Brackenbeck we realised that we had something very special in terms of photographic evidence. But quite naturally, any claims by anyone of the appearance of anything unusual or paranormal on photographs often raises sceptical eyebrows and a whole array of questions as to whether the images may be misidentifications, tricks of the light, hoaxes or camera faults. There is nothing wrong with a healthy scepticism, it is a vital part of any researchers' mental tool kit; and when balanced by an open enquiring mind, it can often lead us to the truth. Sceptical enquiry is important in any field of study; the debunker, however is a different kettle of fish. As anyone involved in any kind of extraordinary or paranormal phenomena knows, there is always a professional debunker lying around somewhere ready to snipe at anyone who sticks their head above the orthodox parapet!

Unlike the normal sceptic, a debunker does not have an open mind, he usually has his mind already firmly made up; in spite of the evidence; and uses every means possible to slant the facts towards the bias of his own hidden agenda, whatever that may be.

In this chapter we shall look at some of the explanations usually trotted out by those whose remit it is to debunk claims of paranormal activity; particularly with reference to strange anomalous images such as orbs and luminosities. We shall then examine a few of our own photographs and see what they can tell us.

From the start we were quite open-minded about our phenomena, and willing to look at any reasonable explanations, be they normal or paranormal. But before we review some of the usual explanations for luminosities on digital images, let's take a brief look at photography in general.

Photography was pioneered by a Frenchman, Joseph N. Niepce, who made the first true photograph on a metal plate in 1826. He and Louis Daguerre then developed the photographic process in 1829 and by 1839 Daguerre had produced the first daguerrotype; an impression made on a light-sensitive silver-coated metallic plate and developed by mercury vapour. This was the forerunner of all later photographic processes. And for almost two centuries there has been a continual advancement in photographic image-making, with individuals and companies striving to create better equipment and processes. But with the advent of micro chips the photographic world changed. Today, what is in effect a revolutionary technology, has become commonplace for most of us. Nowadays digital cameras, even low cost entry level models, can give near photographic quality images. And as a myriad of websites now testify, the majority of orbs are captured by digital cameras.

But, of course, anomalous photographic images are nothing new. Back in the early days of photography, as it became more popular and sophisticated, a whole array of strange anomalous images started to appear on a wide cross section of photographs and negatives. A percentage were obviously due to the inexperience of would be photographers but some seemed to be quite inexplicable in normal terms. Such cases naturally enough caused quite a deal of controversy at the time. Last century, one of the most famous, or infamous, depending on your point of view; was the case of the Cottingley Fairies.

Briefly: this involved two young cousins, Elsie Wright and Frances Griffiths, who in 1917 took photographs of fairies they'd reputedly seen in Cottingley Glen, near Bradford. At the time Elsie was fifteen and Frances ten years old. It was Sir Arthur Conan Doyle, the creator of Sherlock Holmes, who brought this case to public attention in an article published in the 1920 Christmas edition of Strand Magazine. Coincidently, Conan Doyle had already been commissioned by the editor to write an article on fairies for the Christmas issue, which he was already working on in June when he first saw the Cottingley photographs. They were brought to Sir Arthur's attention and ultimately to the publics' by a Theosophist named, Edward Gardener.

Since 1917 the girl's photographs had been hidden away in a drawer, only coming to light three years later when Elsie's mother passed them on to Gardener for examination in 1920. Since the Strand article, controversy has raged as to whether or not these photographs are genuine. Mystifyingly, though Conan Doyle championed their credibility, he never actually met the girls himself; and, also rather strangely, no one thought to examine the original photographs either, all seeming content to analyse prints! And to put it into context both Conan Doyle and Edward Gardner were not unbiased, being already convinced believers in the realm of nature spirits. Those less biased pointed out that these fairies had currently fashionable hairstyles and looked suspiciously similar to images found in fairy tale books of the period. The debate continued and the girls kept quiet.

From 1941 to 1972 Gardeners' own book: 'The Cottingley Photographs and their Sequel' went through many editions. But by 1945 the Theosophical Society, who had originally authenticated the Cottingley photographs, were themselves getting sceptical of the images. Later research on the photographs rather suggested that although Conan Doyle may have been the creator of Sherlock Holmes, in this instance, he didn't evidence the same powers of detection. Four out of the five images of the fairies looked like card or paper cut-outs. For those who did not believe in fairies, these alleged photographs of fairies just had to be fakes.

But in spite of sceptical prodding, neither Elsie nor Frances, who both died in the last decades of the 20th century, ever jointly admitted that the photographs were faked. And although some claim that the girls at last admitted to the hoax, a reading of the transcripts of the 1971 BBC Nationwide interview and Austin Mitchell's interview for Yorkshire Television in September 1976, reveals that this is not exactly the case. Though, any hints of fakery were seized on with great glee by a great many sceptics.

In her last television appearance in 1986 Frances maintained that; 'there were fairies at Cottingley'. And indeed, as yet, no one has conclusively proved that the photographs were faked.

What happened to the photographs? Well, in March 2001 Bonhams & Brooks of Knightsbridge, offered for auction: 'The whole collection of glass plates and photographic negatives by the first Cottingley researcher, Edward Gardener.'

This 84-year old photographic archive of the famous Cottingley Fairies, including previously unpublished plates of Elsie and Frances; and other examples of 19th and 20th century spirit photography, fetched £6,000 at auction; the whole collection being bought by an anonymous buyer. But whether or not this may shed any more light on the Cottingley case is anybody's guess!

As well as promoting the Cottingley fairies, Sir Arthur Conan Doyle was also an advocate of the cause of spiritualism, which in those days was also greatly advanced by the new art of photography. The camera provided spiritualists with a whole new phenomena; 'spirit photography'. Interestingly, after his death in 1930, Conan Doyle, himself, became a common subject for spirit photographers to summon up; though one such ghostly photograph of Sir Arthur; appears to be a reversed cut-out placed on cotton wool. Unfortunately many other popular examples of spirit photography later proved to be fakes, created by those wishing to fleece the gullible. At the time this caused bad publicity for genuine researchers into the paranormal. However, over the years, many authentic photographs of strange light phenomenon have been taken accidentally by ordinary people, with no particular beliefs or agendas.

As mentioned earlier, those who believe such photographic light anomalies to be manifestations of paranormal activity usually categorise them as: orbs, vapours, vortices or apparitions, with orbs probably now being the most commonly photographed anomaly.

Orbs themselves are relatively recent as photographic phenomena; occurring more frequently since the advent of digital photography. Over the past few years orbs have become quite popular and have featured in articles, books and documentaries on the paranormal. In fact whilst writing this book, a TV programme dealing with psychic abilities, mentioned orbs as a common phenomenon; and a friend reported that her neighbours had recently photographed orbs, when their little boy said there was something odd in his room!

As we pointed out previously, it does seem rather odd that even with today's affordable and technologically sophisticated cameras, the occurrence of spheres, disks and other orb-like photographic anomalies have actually increased.

One would have thought they would have decreased! Surely the better photographic technology becomes, the less likely it is for photographic anomalies to crop up at all. Or is new technology giving us all the ability to capture something that was always there but just not previously or commonly photographable?

To all intents and purposes it would seem that people all over the world are actually photographing a real phenomenon!

Sceptics will no doubt initially find this an incredible sweeping assumption, but discounting the even more unlikely possibility of a consistent worldwide malfunction in every type of digital camera, what other non-paranormal causes could there be?

It seemed to us that there are two areas of probability: natural causes, such as rain, mist, dust, water droplets, sunlight, insects, or technical causes, such as digital errors, pixel blocks, flash reflection and lens flare. We ourselves avoid trying to photograph orbs in the rain or in wet, misty or dusty conditions, to minimise the possibility of atmospheric causes.

The most common explanation offered by sceptics is that of lens flare caused by direct sunlight or another hard light source hitting the lens. Flare can certainly sometimes project the shape of the aperture opening and create rings of light on a photograph. Some purported orbs may indeed be nothing more than the familiar light circles due to lens flare. But this is definitely not the case in terms of the vast majority of luminosities that people have photographed.

Most orbs for instance, tend to be photographed either indoors or in dark or dim conditions where sunlight or any other light source entering the lens is not a valid possibility. A small percentage of orbs are undoubtedly due to flash reflections, or lens flare but these are pretty obvious effects and such images will quickly be discounted by those seriously interested in photographing the phenomena. And as mentioned above, digital errors and processing anomalies seems very unlikely considering the worldwide nature of the phenomena.

So how would you recognise a genuine orb or luminosity?

Well, most people will know if it was raining or not, or if the sun was hitting the lens, or if they were standing in a cloud of gnats etc. when they took a photograph that later showed up something odd. If you are an ordinary honest person of reasonable intelligence, it is very probable that you will know when you have photographed a genuine orb or luminosity.

As a general rule though, orbs, when photographed, usually take the form of disc or sphere-like objects, which more often than not appear lighter than the background image. Luminosities and sphere-like anomalies tend to be mainly white, often with tints of blue or pink, whilst many other orbs appear as faceted disk-like structures that may cover all the colours of the spectrum. So far, orbs have been recorded in all kinds of numbers from one to well over 200 in a single photograph!

At a casual glance it may seem that some orbs, such as a few we ourselves have taken, look similar to the refracted sunlight caused by lens flare. We noted this slight similarity on several images ourselves but realised that sunlight wasn't a viable cause because those same images had been taken at dusk or in the dark.

Orbs often appear in close proximity to people and have been noted to specifically congregate in areas where emotions have been intensely active. Some would also say they are drawn to people who emanate psychic energy. Certainly with internet access and file sharing, the ubiquitous occurrence of orbs has given rise to a worldwide interest in this subject.

Discounting obvious natural and technical causes, the photographic evidence suggests that something extraordinary is happening all over the world. In looking for answers to our own phenomenon we had already exhausted all the obvious possible indoor causes, such as reflections. We have a large kitchen with lots of reflective surfaces and objects and yet have not managed to get more than two shots of orbs in there, even though over the years we've taken lots of photographs of friends and family fooling about or happily tucking in. If orbs are merely reflected light effects we would have certainly got them in the kitchen. In our experience it's unlikely that reflections always equal orbs. This is well demonstrated by comparing

the following two photographs.

First, look at photograph 19. This shows a few typical orbs in our front room. The fireguard is for the benefit of visiting relatives who were there with their child at

the time. The reflection in the mirror is from the light fitting hanging from the ceiling. But in case you're tempted to think that perhaps the orbs in the foreground are the result of light reflection; compare this photograph

with the next one, taken only seconds later. It is approximately the same angle of shot, the same lighting conditions and same camera settings but, hey - no orbs.

For those tempted to write orbs off as nothing more than light reflections, this comparison is worth bearing in mind.

Now, let's return to photo 3 in Chapter 1. Did you spot the critical factor?

The orb is behind Sam's head! This completely cancels out the idea that orbs are only camera lens effects. They are certainly not in this instance.

Both reflection and light refraction anomalies will only produce effects in front of the background image. Orbs captured behind people or objects are obviously not an anomaly created within the camera lens. If orbs show up as being clearly behind any elements in a photograph then this fact indicates that they are in all probability actual objects in the outside world. And Photo 3 is not the only example of this. (Photo 21) shows an orb behind the

coal scuttle in the front room. And the next photograph taken in the garden, shows an orb behind leaves. (Photo. 22.).

These are fairly typical of the shots we have taken in which orbs appear behind some thing or someone. Again we must stress, anything that is behind elements in a photograph clearly suggest that it is part of the real world outside of the camera. Consequently orbs must, if only for a microsecond, be part of the visible light spectrum to be photographed at all – and as such they must be real objective phenomenon.

Being designers we are very aware of light and colour and had both felt from early on that there had to be some objectively real visual element involved here, something more than just odd lighting effects or digital camera glitches. As we continued with our photo-expeditions in the grounds of Brackenbeck we were increasingly impressed with the physicality of the phenomena. Look at how on the

next photograph: (Photo. 23.) the nearer orbs are brighter and sharper whilst the ones further away in the trees are dimmer and more distant looking. Just as you would expect if taking a photograph of an actual physical phenomena that had individual elements at varying distances from the camera.

This is an effect we often saw in many shots of orbs outdoors. Whether or not orbs are non-physical phenomena invisible to the naked eye, once photographed they often appear to have definite physical properties, such as perspective. Neither lens flare nor sunlight can account for this and it's highly unlikely that digital camera faults will selectively give perspective to some elements on a photograph without distorting the rest of the image. In trying to determine what it was we were photographing, we had to thoroughly consider all the aforementioned obvious natural causes. We did tests to eliminate these: we deliberately photographed rain, leaves, bubbles, pollen, insects; we'd even thrown up dust and photographed that. Mostly we got nothing, but if we did, it looked nothing at all like the luminosities we were photographing. This is something you could try yourself, if you have photographed orbs before, just try to replicate them. It's quite instructive.

As we continued photographing orbs both indoors and outdoors, with flash, without flash, in daylight and at night time, we could see no consistent and obvious factor present that could cause the orbs to appear where they did, or as often as they did.

One evening we photographed some luminosities outside our front door, floating over the drive. (Photo. 24.)

This photograph demonstrates the perspective effect of both near and distant objects. Some of these seem to have a motion blur, as though they were caught moving. In all our own images any camera faults would have shown up repeatedly everywhere else. They didn't. And other normal explanations such as sunlight, flash reflection, or all the other natural causes we have already mentioned, had been shown to be either not relevant at the time, not consistent with what we were photographing or highly improbable in the circumstances!

Our comparisons of various common factors that may give rise to orb-like images have convinced us that none of the usual explanations fit the events. We had to look in other directions to discover what mechanism was at work to make it possible for us to photograph this fascinating phenomenon.

Critical Angles:

Question: Do natural explanations such as lens flare, flash feedback, reflections, rain, mist, dust, insects, etc. adequately explain the appearance of orbs and luminosities on photographic images?

Answer: No.

Question: Does the fact that orbs and other luminosities appear on photographs at all, both in front of and behind objects, suggest that they must be present in the visual spectrum in order to be photographed, and as such are very likely to be part of the external world beyond the camera?

Answer: Yes!

CHAPTER 6

WHAT IS SCIENTIFIC AND WHAT IS NOT

"For the public, a better understanding of the nature of science would lead to their regarding scientists with less awe and a dash more scepticism. A more realistic attitude would be healthy for both."

WILLIAM BROAD and NICHOLAS WADE,
Betrayers of the Truth

Anyone involved with paranormal phenomena will often be viewed with suspicion by scientists and academics. And with complete scepticism by those of a dogmatic mindset who cling to the skirts of the nursemaids of orthodoxy that protect them from the disturbing anomalies that exist at the fringes of 'normality'. So, before we move on in our account we would like to look briefly at something that concerns every one of us who is interested in what lies beyond the edge of what is commonly acceptable in terms of the prevailing view of science.

What is scientific and what is not?
Science could be simply described as a method for exploring and investigating the universe. As any good explorer knows, if you are in unknown territory you have to take your bearings to know where you are in relation to everything else around you. Even in the middle of some unknown locality we can usually do this by fixing our bearings

on things we recognise, such as the position of the sun, the familiar shape of hills in the distance, or the stars in the sky. This gives us a rough mental map of where we are and what may be the best direction in which to travel. Anyone who sets out to explore or investigate the cosmos around them needs some sort of mental map of the universe he or she is investigating. These mental reference maps are known as 'paradigms'. Until the time of Copernicus, astronomers had used Ptolemy's concept that the Earth was at the centre of everything with the sun, stars and planets all neatly revolving around it, as their map of the universe. This was the prevailing viewpoint of that time, and so Ptolemy's Earth-centred universe could be said to be the scientific paradigm of its day.

As history testifies, both religious and scientific paradigms are apt to change, though this isn't usually a quick process. In general people are as reluctant to let go of their old familiar paradigms, as they are of letting go of some favourite old jumper. Usually they try to hang on to them as long as possible. Of course, real science should be all about discovering truth, which it is in essence; but sometimes it just doesn't seem that way. Occasionally old scientific theories can change almost overnight but more often than not it takes a long time for change to occur; especially if new knowledge runs contrary to the orthodox viewpoint.

No matter how good one piece of evidence may be it sometimes takes a long time for new views to become acceptable.

What is considered valid science; often depends on the prevailing paradigm. History is littered with accounts of scientific orthodoxy ignoring or suppressing new evidence that did not fit cherished theories. When a scientific hypothesis has been confirmed enough times, it often takes on the status of a law, such as the law of magnetism or the law of gravity. In science such laws are very important in describing predictive phenomena; but the fact is these laws do not always explain the phenomena they describe. In magnetism, for example, the law that like magnet poles repel each other and unlike poles attract each other does not explain why this is so, only that it happens. Often the public are under the mistaken impression that such laws are absolutes; like the Ten Commandments, when in fact they are merely descriptive tools to aid understanding. This mistaken view of science is why scientific theories, like religious dogma, is sometimes used like a sledgehammer to bludgeon to death the things people feel threatened by.

Science is often described as being totally unbiased and objective, like some kind of absolute standard of truth. We go contrary to it at our peril. But science is no more unbiased or objective than humanity is always honest or truthful. Objectivity and truthfulness are qualities that rationally can only be applied to individuals and then only within certain limits. Realistically only individual scientists can be said to be objective or truthful. And of course, here lies the thorn in the side of scientific objectivity. As individuals it is not possible for any of us to be totally objective, no more than it is possible for people to tell 'the truth, the whole truth and nothing but the truth' when asked to swear to that effect on oath in a court of law. It is literally beyond the capabilities of human beings with fallible memories, whose interpretation of events is always subjective. The 'whole truth' is something literally outside of the experience of any individual.

In terms of the law and science then, truth; considering the limitations of even the most honest person; often has to be the best approximation in the circumstances. As we tried to find the truth behind our own luminosity phenomena we found it more difficult to reconcile what we had experienced with what we had learned of current physics. There was definitely an aspect to the phenomena that inclined us more towards the metaphysical and paranormal as likely areas of investigation. Like many before us, we were now in danger of stepping over the borderline into that dubious area some would consider as pseudo-science.

But just what is pseudo-scientific!

It seemed to us that, depending on your perspective, it is one of two things:

a) scientific jargon used to justify conclusions that have been arrived at without reference to all the known facts or recourse to any scientific method. Or,

b) a reasonably feasible theory based on all the known evidence, but which does not fit with the prevailing viewpoint of scientific orthodoxy.

Interestingly the latter was just the area that the Wright Brothers found themselves in when, over two years after they had made their first flight, certain scientists of the day were still writing papers proving that it was scientifically impossible for objects heavier than air to fly! I wonder what they would have thought of jumbo jets.

Those who look into any phenomenon that strays beyond the boundaries of the accepted paradigm of the day, inevitably find themselves at odds with scientific orthodoxy, their ideas and theories being usually labelled as cranky or pseudo-scientific. However, the history of science itself is not a pure example of objective truthfulness. On occasion, scientists have been known to actively deny real phenomena that did not conform to current scientific thinking. Take meteorites, for example. If you sit out in the countryside on a clear night and watch the sky for long enough there is a good chance that you will see a shooting star. Of course what you see is not a star at all but a tiny particle of cosmic debris that flashes briefly as it burns up in our atmosphere. Usually these are meteors disintegrating through atmospheric friction. It's estimated that somewhere around 100 million of them enter our atmosphere every day. The larger chunks that don't burn up, but sometimes impact the Earth, are known as meteorites. These range in size from pebbles to huge rocks weighing tons. Fortunately your chances of winning the National Lottery are over a hundred million times greater than being struck by a meteorite!

Today most of us are familiar with comets and meteorites. We know that they are natural cosmic phenomena. We no longer take them as signs or omens from the gods. But it wasn't so long ago that people did. For hundreds of years iron meteorites that fell to earth were preserved in temples, believed to have been sent by the gods.

It was the iron from meteorite impacts that ancient metallurgists used to forge the iron weapons that gave their bearers dominance over those who still used weapons of bronze. When it came to warfare, as history testifies, it was often metal from the stars that decided the fate of nations on Earth.

Ironically, after the Renaissance and the establishment of scientific rationalism, for many years accounts of meteorites falling to Earth were dismissed by the scientists of the day as nothing more than the superstitious beliefs of the ignorant.

The prevailing scientific logic of the day dictated that stones could not possibly fall from the sky because there were no stones in the sky. Ipso facto, meteorites therefore did not, could not, possibly exist. In spite of many well documented observations of meteorites, scientific sceptics were so convinced that rocks could not possibly fall from the sky that they instigated a concerted effort to have meteorite fragments removed from museums and collections or destroyed.

Today, of course, with a wider perspective and understanding of our cosmic environment; meteorites and meteors are accepted as a natural astronomical phenomenon, that regularly enters the Earth's atmosphere. There are two types of meteors; sporadic, which can appear at any time; and shower meteors, which only appear at certain times of year. The best known of the meteor showers is the Leonid shower, so called because it radiated from the direction of the constellation of Leo. Leonids appear in mid-November each year and are well worth watching for. Between the years 1833 and 1866 tremendous showers of Leonids were seen, thousands per hour raining across the sky. Some fundamentalists saw them as fulfilment of the Bible's words about falling stars in Matthew. 24:29 and Revelation 6:13, but of course, these were not stars at all, just the meteors that science had affirmed did not exist.

Such great numbers have not been seen since then because the orbit of the Leonids has shifted, but it was the amazing occurrence of the great meteor showers of the late 19th century that prompted scientists to put aside their preconceptions and begin to properly investigate the phenomena; which of course, they did.

But often as history shows, the much-vaunted rationality of science has in many instances been overstated to the point where science is seen as the only rational use of the human intellect. And quite naturally, in psychological terms, some scientists have played up to this; putting themselves forward as the arbiters of reason to an irrational public. But this is not all the fault of science; leaders and politicians have often put scientists in the unenviable position of being the exclusive guardians of knowledge and reason in society.

As far as scientists as individuals go, question marks as to their total genuineness, hang over many notable names in the annals of science, from ancient Greece to the present day and include such names as: Claudius Ptolemy, Galileo Galilei and even Isaac Newton! Unfortunately as history testifies; the wheels of orthodoxy, scientific or otherwise, shift but slowly in new directions. And no doubt many scientists today would cast the whole idea of orbs, spheres, ghost lights, ball lightning and other luminosities into the outer darkness, along with: the Loch Ness monster, the flat earth and leprechauns - not to mention angels and faeries!

Whilst certain individual scientists have often been scathingly critical of spiritual perspectives and biased against paranormal phenomena, we must not make the mistake of writing off all scientists as being blinkered – this is not true of scientists in general nor is it true of science itself. Many of the benefits we take for granted in our modern world would not be available to us if it were not for persistent and methodical scientific research. Science originally arose out of people asking philosophical questions about the nature of existence, and it is the best tool we have for the rational investigation of the universe. Though sometimes, like all tools, it can be bent by those who wield it.

Our problem was not how to make our explanations acceptable to current scientific thinking, but how to understand our phenomena. How to explain it as reasonably as we could; in terms of what we knew of its aspects and behaviour. And if this proves too incredible or controversial for some, then there is very little we can do about it, except to encourage others to look into the matter of luminosities themselves.

For most of those involved in investigating the rich spectrum of extraordinary things and paranormal events, exploring the universe is about more than making the facts fit current perceptions. It is about trying to understand what the mysterious anomalies rejected by orthodoxy may actually mean in relation to everything else we know; and just sometimes this may lead us toward new horizons.

Critical Angles:

Question: If, as history shows, that prevailing scientific paradigms have been flawed in the past, is it probable that the current paradigm is also flawed?

Answer: Yes.

Question: Is it possible that scientific perceptions of paranormal phenomena in general, are conditional to an incomplete understanding of the universe?

Answer: Yes.

CHAPTER 7

SEEING THE LIGHTS

"Umbra: (n) the area in a shadow from which light is completely cut off."

(LONGMAN'S ILLUSTRATED SCIENCE DICTIONARY)

"Light: n. electromagnetic radiation by which things are visible;"

(COLLINS POCKET ENGLISH DICTIONARY)

It was not long after we first started photographing our luminosities, that we came to realise that sometimes Katie could actually see something before a photo of an orb was taken. What Katie saw were small flashes of light. The first instance of this was one afternoon when she was about to take a shot of a new painting she'd just hung up. She noticed a flash of neon pink light by the wall opposite the fireplace. Instinctively she took a shot in that direction and the result-

ing photograph showed a large smudgy luminosity. (Photo.25.) Below it was a smaller one on the floor.

A few days later Katie was again in the front room in the late afternoon when she saw what she later described as a brief pulse of light on the wall near to the door. I was present this time but saw nothing.

We had just come in from taking some

shots outside and her camera was still on.

She took a shot in the direction of the light before I had time to say anything. When we looked at it on screen, there was definitely a luminosity where she had seen the light and it had what appeared to be a motion trail. (Photo. 26.)

It looked just as if it had zoomed in through the solid door! But as we know, appearances can be deceptive. If orbs are non-physical phenomena, what appears to be a motion trail may be nothing of the kind. We already suspected, as some of our photographs seemed to indicate, that the cats could sometimes see the orbs we were photographing. Could the lights Katie had seen actually be visible luminosities?

If so this was a very exciting development for us. Especially in the light of the fact that for several years Katie herself had experienced a strange visual phenomenon, which up to that point she had only seen but never before photographed.

Because this relates directly to the luminosities that are the subject of this book, we shall take a step back in time and briefly relate how Katie came to experience what we have now termed, 'Small Transient Lights phenomenon', or STL, for short.

Katie's experience of these strange lights began about ten years earlier, before I'd even met her. At the time, although Katie was living in a charming 400 year old converted cottage; she was very unhappy both in her personal relationship and in her working life. Added to which, the old cottage appeared to be haunted. Odd noises and disturbing physical effects only served to compound Katie's feelings of helplessness in a situation she couldn't seem to resolve. Almost instinctively she began to reach out, in her thoughts, to a higher power; though she could put no name to it as she didn't follow any particular religious path.

Lying in bed at night, she would try to rise above her troubles and let her spirit fly free; seeking something that she instinctively felt was there for her. Though she didn't know it at the time, she was beginning to journey along the same path through the dark that seekers from all time have followed, each one carrying their own small individual lamps of hope to light their way.

Though feeling lost herself, Katie was an inherently kind and giving personality, and so she began to concentrate on sending out thoughts of love and hope to others who may also be lost in the dark. Each night as she reached out to the universe or god or whatever good powers there were, she sought connection and guidance. Then the lights began to appear!

The very first time she saw one, it was in the corner of the front room at the old cottage. It looked like a little star, twinkling briefly and then vanishing. It was to be the first of many such occurrences. Soon Katie was seeing them regularly. Tiny, neon pink, purple or blue lights that flashed momentarily on walls, in darkened corners or around people, even on her work, sometimes singularly, sometimes in clusters. The little lights varied, some were brighter and longer lasting than others. Katie found their appearance more comforting than disturbing, although as a designer who depended on her eyes to earn her living, it was rather worrying what this phenomena may forebode. She made appointments to get her eyesight checked.

Both her doctor and optician were concerned when she explained about the lights, but after all the usual tests the doctor could find nothing physiologically wrong. The optician was perplexed. Katie's eye tests were all normal. The best diagnosis he could offer was what he jokingly called being 'star struck'. He told her not to worry. There was no physical problem with her vision, although he had to admit, that he'd never met anyone else who saw these strange lights.

However this phenomenon is not unique to Katie.

Many people world wide experience it. Small Transient Lights phenomena (STL) is often seen by mediums, psychics and healers but it is also common in the experience of many ordinary people who make no claims at all of paranormal phenomenon. In the majority of instances it is usually so insubstantial that many choose to ignore it or subconsciously forget it is there, like the floaters in our eyes which we only see if we concentrate on them.

It may be that you too have seen these little lights, flashing in a micro second burst of light or twinkling around people you meet? There is nothing wrong with your eyes; what you are seeing is exactly the same phenomenon that Katie sees; and it is there all the time; all we have to do is look! When you see them, if you're quick enough, try using your digital camera to take a shot in that direction; sooner or later you are sure to photograph orbs.

For Katie, STL became an intermittent but recurring phenomenon that didn't seem to have any particular pattern to it. Though it did have meaning! The appearance of the lights had now set her feet on a new path that was quietly but inexorably leading her out of the grip of those things that had been stifling her spirit. Looking back it seems to us both, that the lights themselves had been an answer to Katie's dilemma and to her reaching out in the dark for guidance.

During the next four years Katie was on her own journey of discovery. She had begun to wonder if other people also saw these little lights?

Katie was now quite used to seeing the lights and had accepted them as part of her life. She even felt comforted by their periodic appearances and began to feel that perhaps there was a purpose to them. Was there a connection between the little lights and the people they appeared around; could it be that they were responding to emotional states? Were they a phenomenon generated by the psyche of others; or were they a sign of some kind of empathy between her self and another?

As Katie searched for answers this inevitably led towards changes; opening up her life in a new and positive way. One day, a friend at work suggested she try going for an aromatherapy massage. Katie had never done anything like that before. The aromatherapist had a consulting room in a rather bleak old mill building; the last place Katie would have thought to find anyone involved in the healing arts. She was at first a bit discouraged by the surroundings, but as soon as Katie stepped inside the aromatherapy room she instantly saw a multitude of tiny white lights. They filled the air at the far end of the softly lit room. She'd never before seen so many at once. She'd hardly taken the next breath when they vanished.

The aromatherapy room had a warm positive feel to it and as the session progressed Katie felt a kinship with Hanna, the aromatherapist; and told her of the lights which she had seen on entering the room. Hanna explained that she had often seen them herself. Katie was instantly attentive; it was the first time she'd ever met anyone else who'd seen the little lights, and was eager to hear more. Hanna thought they were some kind of healing energies working alongside her. Katie was overjoyed to discover that she wasn't the only one seeing the little twinkling lights, and that they were evidently a real objective phenomenon. It was a turning point in her understanding. Within the next month Katie got a management position with a new company and moved away from the area; but not away from her lights. They accompanied her wherever she went. Some months after settling in at her new job, she and her best friend, Wendy, set off for an introductory evening of Ti Chi taken by Jason Chan. In a community hall there was a mixture of people of various ages and backgrounds all standing with knees bent, learning how to breathe and be one with the chi energy.

Tai Chi exercises the body, soothes the mind and lifts the spirit. It is like meditation in motion. Interestingly the symbol for Tai Chi is a circle. Most people will know this as the familiar Yin and Yang symbol, in which two semicircles, one light, the other dark, meet each other to form a complete circle. In Chinese symbolism this is literally called the 'Tai Chi'; and it perfectly symbolises the spirit of Tai Chi, which is mind and body balanced and moving in harmony.

After the session had finished Wendy and Katie decided to listen to the conversations. Katie was especially interested in one man in particular who was describing little lights he'd been seeing for several years. They sounded just like the lights that Katie saw. She listened attentively. He wondered why he didn't see them anymore; he felt less without them and wanted to see them again. What could he do? Jason just told him to keep on looking. Katie had never thought about not ever being able to see her little lights again.

She was pondering on this on the way out, when Wendy excitedly informed her that she too had just seen lots of little white lights as they stepped outside. Though she knew about Katie's lights, this was the first time Wendy had seen them herself. They were both delighted and wondered if it was the effect of the Tai Chi. But whatever it was, Katie was very happy that her best friend was now able to share this with her. Katie had already seen an amazing amount of small neon pink lights in the room that night and felt totally energised.

She said Goodbye to Wendy, but after a couple of miles of travelling homeward all the electrics on her car suddenly cut out. Luckily it was a clear starry night with not much traffic about. Realising that Katie was not behind her, Wendy, drove back to see what had happened. Neither of them are helpless females who know nothing about cars and in the next ten minutes they had tried all the basic procedures, but there was not a peep of power, the car was dead as the proverbial dodo.

Katie, suddenly saw a white light over the steering wheel! She turned the key again. This time the engine instantly started! Incidentally, her car never had electrical failure before or since! Katie couldn't help but wonder if she'd been so super charged with Chi energy that night that it had actually affected the electrics in the car? Impossible! Or is it?

In the Eastern tradition, Chi is a universal energy, as immediate as thought itself. In Hindu philosophy this energy is called prana; and here a distinction is made between physical and psychic prana; which may account for certain aspects of our light phenomena, such as the difference in scale between Katie's small transients lights; the photographable orbs and the larger luminosities. Later we shall look at how this universal energy may have a connection with Katie's recurring transient lights and with the occurrence of luminosities and other phenomena.

Critical Angles:

Question: Is the Small Transient Lights phenomena photographable?

Answer: Yes.

Question: Is it possible that Small Transient Lights Phenomena may be a visual aspect of the orbs phenomenon?

Answer: Yes!

CHAPTER 8

FIREBALLS AND PLASMA THEORY

From the throne came flashes of lightning, rumblings and peals of thunder.

REVELATION 4. 5.

'Look!' said one. 'The lights again! Last night the watchmen saw them start and fade from midnight until dawn. Something is happening up there.'

J.R.R. TOLKIEN, *The Hobbit.*

Inexplicable spheres of light! Thunderbolts and fireballs from the sky!

As the hammer of Thor beats upon the dome of heaven, even now an age-old controversy sets fire in the eyes of sceptics and believers alike. Whatever you may believe about it, hundreds of sightings have been made over the centuries of the fiery celestial phenomenon commonly known as ball lightning. The evidence for its existence now seems irrefutable; and yet some scientists still deny its existence.

But the main point of debate now is what actually causes ball lightning in the first place and how does it work?

As we considered our own phenomena, we wondered if it was possible that our luminosities could be connected in some way to the forces responsible for ball lightning. Our latest research into the subject had raised that possibility and there was already a viable theory to that effect known as; plasma theory. Was it possible there could be a connection between plasma energy, ball lightning and orbs?

Before we explore that possibility, let us look at what is known of ball lightning itself. There is certainly no shortage of testimony from those who, over the years, have witnessed ball lightning and its effects. But first, the eyewitness account I am most familiar with: my own:

COVERED MIRRORS AND OPEN DOORS

When thunder rolled and the summer storm walked on legs of lightning across the land, my grandmother would always take precautions. She would draw the curtains, cover all the mirrors with tea towels and open the back door. She always left the back door open to let out a thunderbolt in case one came down the chimney. Where she got this custom from I don't know, but it was meant to protect the house against lightning and thunderbolts. Nowadays this may sound a rather silly and superstitious thing to have done, but like much folklore and superstition it was founded on fact.

To a boy of nine, thunderbolts sounded both exciting and frightening though I had no idea what a thunderbolt actually was. Not until I saw one. It was August, my grandmother and I were sheltering in the backroom as the electric storm boomed and flashed over the valley. She had taken all her usual precautions and the interior of the house was dim behind the drawn curtains. Suddenly, in the darkened room, there was an intense glow of light. Right by the front of the fireplace, just as though it had come down the chimney, was an amazing ball of shimmering blue light. I remember it being about the size of a football, perhaps a little larger. Floating about a foot or so off the floor, it seemed to ripple, like something seen through a summer heat haze. The luminous sphere seemed to be wobbling slightly as it glided slowly towards the settee. My grandmother quickly grabbed me and pulled me to the other side of the room. Wide eyed we watched it from behind the big polished oak table. I can recall an acrid smell and the air seemed to tingle. I remember feeling that prickling sensation known as 'pins and needles' dancing all over my skin. The ball of bluish light had now drifted around the settee, stopping for a few moments in front of the glass china cabinet, just as though looking at its own reflection. I watched it, half in fear; half in fascination. Moments later it glided through the doorway and into the kitchen. Extricating myself from my grandmother's grip, I cautiously followed just in time to see it exit the house through the back door.

Running outside I looked vainly around but the ball of light had disappeared; apparently swallowed up by the storm that had brought it! For whatever reasons, my grandmother's precautions had worked; the thunderbolt had obligingly left the house through the open back door.

It was an amazing experience, one of those magical childhood memories that has stayed with me over the years, but as yet I've never seen ball lightning again.

A WORLDWIDE PHENOMENON

The phenomenon of ball lightning is well recorded all across the world. Opinions vary as to what exactly causes this and a whole range of other luminous aerial light phenomena known variously as: fire balls, thunderbolts, globe lightning or kugelblitz (when indoors), wildfire, Will-o-the-wisp, Jack-o-lantern or earth lights (when outside). The phenomenon of ball lightning has divided the scientific community since the early 19th century, when the first comprehensive reports came to public notice.

Ball lightning even became the subject of a meeting of the French

Academy of Sciences, where evidence was presented for the appearance of a large number of luminous globes during a tornado in 1890. Eyewitness accounts told of strange luminosities entering houses down chimneys and leaving circular holes through windows as they exited. In spite of many eyewitness accounts of the extraordinary properties of this phenomenon, many members of the Academy poured scorn on it, claiming that witnesses must have been suffering from optical illusions.

In the heated debate that followed, the general consensus was that observations made by uneducated people were valueless. However, sceptic noises were soon muted when the former Emperor of Brazil, a respected foreign member of the Academy, announced that he himself had witnessed ball lightning.

In ancient times ball lightning was seen as a sign from the gods, and has since been classed along side UFOs. It was once thought to be a supernatural phenomenon and was viewed with scepticism by science. Today ball lightning is no longer considered supernatural, although controversy still continues as to what exactly it is.

BALL LIGHTNING AS PLASMA ENERGY

Today the most widely credible explanation for this phenomenon is plasma.

Plasma is; according to the text books, 'an electrically neutral, highly ionised gas, composed of ions, electron and neutral particles.' The air around us always contains both uncharged molecules and molecules of gases which are positively charged. Normally these positively charged particles, known as ions, are widely interspersed, but under unusual conditions, such as in an electric storm, the number of ions may, it is postulated, be increased to form a spontaneous cloud of electrified particles whose reactive motions generate a self-illuminating glow. Plasma! This, according to the theory, is why ball lightning and kindred light phenomena are often associated with electric storms, high voltage power lines or earthquake fault lines, all of which have an electro magnetic effect on the immediate local atmosphere.

Ball lightning is usually seen as a luminous sphere, ranging in diameter from a few inches to a few feet. These spheres are usually orange, red, white or blue in colour and are variously described as: gliding, hovering, floating and drifting. Interestingly, it is also reported as being able to change shape, divide and merge and has been witnessed performing almost instantaneous directional changes and sudden stops. These kinds of manoeuvres would seem to indicate the properties of an essentially weightless and electrically propelled plasma.

Some people claim to have seen ball lightning pass easily through solid surfaces, such as glass or metal, and these luminosities have often been reported entering both buildings and aeroplanes. This too suggests a roving plasma phenomenon.

Reportedly ball lightning can last from a few seconds to a few minutes, sometimes just silently disappearing, sometimes vanishing with explosive force. Whilst the idea of ball lightning as a plasma concentration is now fairly well accepted, the notion that plasma may also be a factor in the orbs phenomenon is less well known. But it was something that we now began to consider.

ORBS AND PLASMA THEORY

The basic premise of the plasma theory as it relates to orbs is that orbs are complex plasma structures, normally invisible to the human eye but sometimes becoming visible when exposed to a large quantity of photons such as are emitted from a camera flash. In this case it is apparently 'fluorescence' that makes orbs photographable. Fluorescence, normally associated with minerals, is the emission of electromagnetic radiation, particularly light, resulting from the irradiation caused by other sources of electromagnetic radiation or particles. Fluorescence persists only as long as the stimulating process continues. The instant you fire a flash; electrons in the plasma concentration move instantaneously to a higher energy orbit when struck by the photons from the light source. When these now highly charged electrons return to their original orbit, new photons (light) are instantly released. All this happens within microseconds and the plasmas are captured as orbs by the fortunate photographer. At least so the theory goes.

This didn't answer for us why Katie was sometimes able to see lights and then photograph luminosities, but it may explain why some orbs in particular appear as flat discs rather than as three-dimensional spheres. Electrons don't form spheres without something to hold them together, such as a dense enough concentration of plasma. Theoretically the plasma concentrations that form orbs have only a minute amount of weight and inertia, which is enough to rapidly propel them in any direction, but not substantial enough during their brief microsecond burst of photon release to form visible spheres. Consequently the electrons simply spread out in all directions, which results in the flat disk-like images captured by the camera at the time of photon bombardment from its flash.

If you are out at night taking flash shots you will sometimes see bright points of light in the air, just after or at the moment the flash goes off. Perhaps pinpointing the usually invisible orb plasmas?

However, ball lightning plasmas, with a higher density and mass, often do form visible spheres. As we studied this topic more we wondered, that if this was true for ball lightning, was it possible that at times, orbs also could form dense enough plasma concentrations to become briefly self luminescent?

Just like ball lightning but much smaller?

Add this to the existing theory that orbs are photographable plasma concentrations and it seemed to explain both aspects of our phenomena: why we could photograph orbs at all, and why Katie sometimes saw a sudden flash of light, prior to us photographing luminosities in the same place. If this was the case, could orbs too, like the larger, ball lightning, also be affected by electromagnetic energy fields?

Under normal weather conditions, ions, (positively charged particles) are randomly dispersed throughout the atmosphere. But during unusual conditions such as a thunderstorm, the number of ions may be rapidly increased and drawn together to form a spontaneous plasma concentration of positively charged electrons.

The plasmas agitated inter-reactive motions then generate a self-illuminating phenomenon. Ball lightning!

If a similar process could also be generated by localised electromagnetic effects nearer to the ground, then smaller and less dense electron-driven plasma concentrations, such as orbs, may be able to become briefly visible without the need for a photon burst from a camera flash at all. This could explain why the cats with optics of unknown range had sometimes appeared to see the orbs on our photographs. So far so good but could plasma theory also explain other luminosities? Perhaps it could.

If a smaller low level plasma concentration had collected a large enough density of positively charged free electrons to self generate photon release, it could then become visible as earth lights, 'will-o-the-wisp' or ghost light phenomena. This may account for certain similarities across a whole range of anomalous light phenomena! Advocates of the plasma idea believe that electric storms have a definite affect on the occurrence of orbs and at the beginning of any electric storm there is a correlation between the density and numbers of orbs appearing.

ORBS BEFORE AND AFTER ELECTRIC STORMS

If the plasma theorists are correct in their basic assumption, that orbs are an electron energy based phenomena, then it is likely they would react to electric storms and to other electromagnetic energy sources. In which case, one would expect distinctly more orbs at the start of a storm than at the end, when the atmospheric energy levels taper off as the storm front dissipates.

We decided to test this out as soon as we had a thunderstorm. Fortunately one arrived the very next week. As we waited for the eye of the storm to reach Brackenbeck, we wondered what effects an electric storm would have on our orbs, if they were, in fact, a plasma phenomenon. Subsequently we twice managed to photograph orbs before and after thunderstorms. But with rather disappointing results,

Before electric storm.   **After electric storm.**

for when comparing the images we could see little difference in the amount of orbs on the photographs taken before a storm and those taken after. We've included two of them in this book so that you can compare the images.

If you have the opportunity it may be interesting to go out and try to photograph images of orbs before and after an electric storm yourself. In spite of our failure to spot any significant differences in this area, you, however, may get better results.

But remember, lightning can be fatally dangerous. Don't take risks.

In general though, the plasma theorists may be right. Obviously many hundreds of photographs would have to be taken in both circumstances before any convincing statistical conclusions could be drawn either way as to whether or not more orbs occur before a storm than after. The fact that orbs can be both seen and photographed means that there has to be some mechanism by which they consistently appear in the visual spectrum. All things considered we felt that the notion of orbs as a plasma phenomenon goes a fair way to explaining their appearance, but it by no means explained all aspects of the phenomena we were experiencing. Other factors were involved here.

Critical Angles:

Question: Does the physical aspects and behaviour of both ball lightning and orbs suggest the possibility that they may both be a plasma phenomenon?

Answer: Yes.

CHAPTER 9

ORBS, DREAMS AND CIRCULAR SYMBOLS

"It is He that sits upon the circle of the earth...that stretches out the heavens as a curtain, and spreads them out as a tent to dwell in."

ISAIAH, 40.22

"Tree circles have appeared in Canada and Czecheslovakia, the trunks bent but not broken."

CAROLYN NORTH, HEALER AND WRITER

"Dreams may contain ineluctable truths, philosophical pronouncements, illusions, wild fantasies, memories, plans, anticipations, irrational experiences, even telepathic visions, and heaven knows what besides. One thing we ought never to forget; almost half our life is passed in a more or less unconscious state."

C. G. JUNG, *The Practical Use of Dream-analysis*

Across the world, as increasing numbers of people found they were photographing orbs; like crop circles, they attracted both human interest and imagination. But unlike the crop circle phenomenon, orbs are much more immediate and available to a wider cross section of people. And wherever they live, people are asking: 'Why am I getting orbs on my photographs? What are they? Do they have meaning?'

Apart from any paranormal considerations, both orbs and circles are re-occurring symbolic forms in the expressions of human consciousness at many levels.

THE SYMBOLOGY OF ORBS

Even in medieval times, European artists were depicting odd circular symbols and orb-like forms; as in Hans Glaser's woodcut of a phenomenon witnessed over Nuremberg on 14 April 1561. (Figure. B.)

Fig. B

Or as in another woodcut that depicts many fiery globes seen over Basel, Switzerland on 7 August 1566 (Figure. C.) Much religious art and architecture includes circles and orbs, as for instance, those depicted in the 13th-century mosaic on the dome of St Mark's in Venice. And of course, the circle of the halo is present in most religious art. The Gnostics also used circular symbolism, as did many other Pre-Christian sects throughout Europe. Orbs, circles and spheres are present in the religious art of ancient Mesopotamia, India, Persia, and China; and even in the art of the ancient

Fig. C

peoples of South America.

And interestingly for us as we researched this subject more, we discovered that quite a few inspirational artists of recent decades, such as, Griselda Tello, in the 1980s, had been including in their art, illustrations of globes and spheres that looked rather orb-like. Were these based on something the artist had actually seen or were they drawn purely from imagination? Are these reoccurring images, in art and prehistory, symbols from the human subconscious? And if so, what do they mean?

Circular and spherical shapes have been widely used to visually express metaphysical concepts and they are also a common occurrence in dreams and visions. Perhaps reflecting the perennial nature of the circle as a fundamental symbolic principle? Circular shapes are not only to be found in the ancient art and pre-historical monuments that are part of our past; they are also the predominant feature in present day crop formations. Something which many see, not only as a modern mythology in the making, but as part of an evolving new spiritual perspective for humanity!

There are many theories from all kinds of viewpoints as to why circular shapes are such universally recurring symbols. The Earth itself can be said to be an orb, sphere or circle. Spheres and circles abound in both astronomy and subatomic physics; atoms move in circular or elliptical orbits; stars and planets are spheroids. Heavenly bodies circle each other and the whole galaxy, of which we are part, rotates through space like a giant wheel, 100,000 light years in diameter. And according to Big Bang theory the whole universe began as a small primordial sphere. We view the world from the orbs of our eyes; and wherever we are, if we turn 180 degrees, we appear to be standing at the centre of a circle!

As a geometric shape the circle was widely used by prehistoric monument builders. Throughout the landscape of Britain and Europe, there is a proliferation of ancient circular structures and formations. And in many areas aerial surveys reveal a landscape covered by a network of circular structures and forms placed there by the unknown circle builders of the past. Upon many monoliths and stone circles, cup and ring marks are familiar symbols, but many stones are also decorated with simple spiral designs. The spiral, a form that winds out from a central point, is a very ancient symbol. Its coiled snake-like form can be seen as representing: the cosmos, energy, evolution or the continuing cycle of life. Throughout our world, since ancient times, the circle has undoubtedly been a universal symbol which has crossed religious and cultural boundaries. Without beginning or end, the circle often represents infinity, perfection and eternity. Greek mathematicians found it an intriguing geometric shape, because although the fixed line that describes its circumference has a finite length, it cannot be calculated exactly and so in one sense can be said to be without end.

Ancient civilisations realised that both human life and the seasons moved in cycles and often depicted the cosmos as a sphere; which is simply a circle in all dimensions.

Structurally spheres contain the maximum volume within the minimum surface area; which is why drops of liquid naturally form into spheres or make spherical shapes.

In Christianity the circle is the symbol of God and also the form of the halo.

The rainbow, which according to Genesis, God set in the sky, is actually a complete circle, although we can usually only see part of it. Another circular emblem familiar to many of us is the Yin Yang symbol. (Figure. D.)

In Chinese this symbol is called "the Tai Chi." In this simple design, two semicircles of light and dark make a complete circle, perfectly symbolising the opposing yet complimentary natures of light and dark, masculine and feminine, positive and negative, at all levels of life. No one knows

Fig. D

who first created this ubiquitous symbol, but it has been embraced by peoples of all religions, and none, as an expression of how they intuitively feel about the circle of life and the balance and harmony within it.

In Tibetan Buddhism the constant cycle of change is symbolised by the circular, Wheel of Life. In the iconography of India the Sanskrit word mandala literally means "circle" and interestingly mandala-like shapes are often spontaneously drawn by people undergoing psychotherapy. In such instances they are thought to represent an expression of the subconscious mind as it seeks for integration of the self. The psychologist Jung was fascinated by mandalas and drew many of his own. Jung came to see the mandala as symbolising transformation.

Mandala motifs can easily be drawn by anyone. (Figure. E.)

Jung believed that drawing mandalas confirmed that the goal of psychic development is the self. As a symbolic outworking of the sub-conscious the mandala became the path to the centre of the individuated

Fig. E

self; the centre of the circle; which Jung saw as the archetype of Oneness. And throughout his work Jung noted that mandalas had a therapeutic effect on the people who drew them.

Indeed it would seem that the circle or sphere is a universal metaphor for wholeness at many levels; even in dreams.

ORBS AND LUMINOSITIES IN DREAMS

Circles, orbs and spheres are recurrent symbols in the dream state and in fact Jung had his own theories about Oneness, synchronistically confirmed by a dream. Nor was Jung the only one to find synchronistic inspiration in a dream, as was demonstrated by a dream recounted by the celebrated atomic scientist, Niels Bohr. When he was a student Bohr had a very strange dream. He saw himself on a ball of burning gas, like the sun. He watched planets whizzing by, whistling as they passed. But though they revolved around the sun they were all attached to it by filaments. Suddenly the gas solidified and the sun and planets all crumbled away. When Niels Bohr awoke he realised that he had just discovered the definitive model of the atom that had so long been sought after by physicists, the 'sun' being the fixed centre around which the electrons revolve. The foundation of atomic physics was built on this dream.

Undoubtedly circles and spheres are powerful symbols for humanity, which is perhaps why we and others find orbs and circles so fascinating. Perhaps they draw us to the centre of our own Oneness? Perhaps this is why today, many people feel drawn to the strange circular symbols of crop formations? There has been much written about the phenomenon of crop circles by other writers and it is not the remit of this book to look at this subject in depth. But what we shall do here is to briefly look at those aspects of crop circles that may possibly relate specifically to our phenomena.

ORBS, LUMINOSITIES AND CROP CIRCLES

Like orbs and luminosities, crop circles appear in many countries of the world, including the UK, Switzerland, Russia, France, Canada, Brazil, the US, New Zealand and Australia. It is highly improbable that the hundreds of designs manifested across the whole globe were made by two old men with boards, as has been claimed in the press and by various professional debunkers. Realistically we have to look for other causes, and this is what occupies the thoughts of crop circle researchers, who have already investigated the most likely natural causes and discounted them. What is left behind is an on going mystery. But what particularly concerns us here is not the finished patterns and designs, but the use of rings and circles in those designs, which demonstrate circular symbolism, and also the numerous reports of mysterious luminosities associated with the actual formation of crop circles.

Some people have tired to make a connection with the strange luminosities associated with crop circles and UFOs. This may or may not be correct, but it seemed to us that the reports in general suggested a light phenomenon that had more in common with earth lights, ball lightning, or with the smaller orb-like concentrations of plasma energy we have already looked at in connection with our own luminosities. Crop circle lights have been variously described as: bright white; yellow, red and orange; even purple; very similar to plasma energies.

As with reports of other luminosities throughout history crop circle lights are said to appear from nowhere; to flash, circle and bob about in the air. This is very like many reports of the way in which both Faerie and ghost lights are said to behave. Take some of the reports of strange lights over fields out of the crop circle context and they would appear to be surprisingly similar to other light phenomena we have mentioned. And just like those other luminosities, crop circle lights are also said to be there one moment and gone the next. Like the faeries of legend, they disappear in the twinkling of an eye.

Sometimes the sightings of crop circle lights have been accompanied by chirping, buzzing or rushing sounds. They have been captured on film and the sounds recorded on tape recorders. Whatever one thinks about what is behind it all, there is little doubt that mysterious luminosities of some kind are associated with crop circle formations. And it is worth mentioning here that in genuine crop circles it has been attested scientifically that the nodes on plants within the circle have been affected physically. In these instances the seeds have been energised to grow at roughly five times the normal rate. But even without this biological evidence, the forces needed to produce complex crop circle designs would have to be both subtle and precise. Many leading researchers believe the indications are that this force is most likely to be electromagnetic. More specifically, research has led some towards the view that plasma energy may be responsible for creating the cellular changes in plants within the circles. Could there be a connection here with the electrically driven plasma energy concentrations that have been postulated as creating ball lightning and causing orbs and other luminosities to self-fluoresce?

Whatever energies are responsible for crop circles and luminosities and whether or not there is a physical connection between the two is still open to question.

But our research has led us to the belief that there is certainly a connection of consciousness; probably even a spiritual connection, with all those symbols of Oneness; whether they manifest as mandalas, crop circles, orbs or luminosities. And it may be possible that all these external circular symbols could even be, as with Jung's mandalas, a synchronistic connecting mechanism between personal and higher consciousness.

As far as our own phenomena went, we at least now had some possible connections between Katie's visible Transient Lights; the photographable orbs; plasma energy concentrations, and the seeming deliberate behaviour on the part of our luminosities. It was at this point that something happened which caused us to consider another possibility; that those same luminosities may also be a connective link between dreams and reality.

THE MEMORY OF A DREAM

Many things can unexpectedly trigger a memory. Sometimes a sight, a sound or a scent can instantly transport us back to the past, our memory suddenly surging into consciousness with a vivid clarity that seems real. For an instant we may relive the taste and feel of a moment from the past. This happened for Katie when one evening we photographed an exceptionally large luminosity in the garden. (Photo. 29.)

It was 2004 and one of the weekends that her friend Wendy had come over to stay. Wendy knew a little about the odd luminosities we were now photographing in the grounds and had bought her own digital camera to try her luck. And indeed she did get a few shots of orbs during that weekend. But one image in particular caught our

attention. (Photo. 30.) This photo showed what looks like a large misty globe between Katie and Wendy. We all studied the image. Wendy thought it looked like a planet, but to Katie the misty orb with its curling vapour instantly recalled a dream she'd had many years ago and for a couple of days she was obviously preoccupied. Talking about it later I learned that during her first pregnancy, Katie was visited by a recurring and disturbing dream.

In her dream she was at all the normal stages of pregnancy; and doing normal things like walking down a street, going shopping, on the beach or in the garden. But wherever she went, always behind her was a large almost transparent misty bubble. She had not thought about the old dream for years, until seeing this particular large luminosity, between her and Wendy. It had instantly recalled the large luminosity in her dream; which had seemed about two feet in diameter and was always behind her, floating about three feet off the ground and approximately 12 feet away. The essence of the dream was that she couldn't escape it. If she darted around a corner, or ran away, every time she looked back; there it was, still at the same distance behind her. If she turned on the spot to face it, she would find it instantly behind her, and at the same distance away. Never once did the bubble-like luminosity appear in front of her. Nor was she ever able to touch it. In her dream she was always in a situation where she was unable to change the outcome. Sadly this symbolical dream proved to be predictive, as Katie later miscarried and lost her first child.

Fortunately Katie was more curious about this image than disturbed by it, as she'd come to terms with her loss long ago, and had subsequently gone on to have two fine sons. But it opened up a new line of enquiry for her.

Had her dream been something from her own subconscious that was trying to prepare her for what was to come? And in the present, could the memories sparked by the photograph be an indication that luminosities had some kind of connectivity with human consciousness; and if so; then to what purpose?

The fact that paranormal phenomena in general, and our own in particular, evidence a high degree of synchronicity for the individuals concerned seemed worthy of further research. Meaningful or predictive dreams have been experienced by many people. Mostly the content is either, personal, mundane or innocuous but predictive dreams are not uncommon. And this in itself suggests that conscious is not confined inside the human skull; it may be connected to a wider external reality.

(We shall look at the question of consciousness and reality later in the book.)

According to dream research, we know that dream encounters with orb-like luminosities and spheres, similar to which Katie experienced are not uncommon. The aspect that Katie found especially worth considering in the circumstances was the fact that her dream was predictive. But if dreams are, as some orthodox psychologists believe, really nothing more than the unconscious imagination driven by the random firing of neurons, the odds against a dream having any sort meaningful significance to real life, outside of the dreamer's head, would be truly astronomical!

But no matter what the sceptics may say, the facts are that people all over the world dream of circular symbols, have predictive dreams and those dreams have meaning. No amount of scepticism persuaded Jung to regard dreams as of no consequence; and as he said: "nobody doubts the importance of conscious experience; why then should we doubt the significance of unconscious happenings?"

Sometimes dreams are uncannily and disturbingly meaningful. Both Katie's dream and the dream of Niels Bohr though totally different, have certain features in common, they both contained spherical symbols and they both had an almost synchronistic relevance to events in the real world. Whatever anyone else may believe about dreams and symbolism, we believed that our orbs and luminosities were part of something that was definitely connected to human consciousness.

Circles and spheres are integral to our existence at practically every level, as fundamental structures in the physical universe, as geometric shapes throughout history and as symbols in the human subconscious. You can't go far in life without bumping into the ubiquitous circles and spheres. They are everywhere!

As an experiment, try counting the numbers of circles and spheres

you encounter daily, in your home, in the office, outside – anywhere you go. Look carefully and you'll be amazed at just how much of your life is made up of, or connected to circular forms.

Leonardo de Vinci had a great interest in symbols and sacred geometry; and in his well-known

Fig. F drawing of the proportions of man

according to Vitruvius, he placed the figure of a man with arms outstretched, at the centre of a circle. (See figure. F)

Perhaps that is where we always are; at the centre of the circle of our own life; turning upon the wheel of experience towards the Oneness within ourselves?

Critical Angles:

Question: Are circles and spheres recurring symbols in nature, in dreams, and in the expressions of human consciousness?

Answer: Yes.

Question: Does the presence of circles or spheres in dreams that relate directly to a personal reality that includes the appearance of circles or spheres, suggest that in these instances they may be some kind of connective link between conscious and unconscious states?

Answer: Yes.

CHAPTER 10

CLOSE ENCOUNTERS WITH LUMINOSITIES

"If the world around us is a world of informational events, the symbolic manifestations that surround UFO reports should be viewed as an important factor "

JACQUES VALLEE

Luminosities, UFOs and paranormal phenomena in general, are not adequately explained in the context of orthodox views of science and physics.

As far as our own luminosities went, we had no instant answers but it seemed likely that like anything else, they had to have some kind of modus operandi that connected them to our reality. No phenomenon, paranormal or otherwise, happens in isolation from the environment in which it occurs. Any event that happens in our reality, is evidently connected to it at some level, even if only briefly. So it was at least possible that some of what we already knew; the

familiar and fundamental principals that make up our everyday reality could cast some light on orbs and luminosities.

Plasma theory seemed at first glance to account for the physics of it all, but as we researched the sub-

ject in a wider context we began to realise that whilst the theory of electrically charged plasma seemed to fit the basic physical aspects, it by no means fully explained the phenomena, especially when such luminosities appear to act with deliberate intent; as when one evening we got a whole room full of orbs in specific response to a comment made by Katie's brother. This was not the only time luminosities had behaved as though they were deliberately interacting with us; for example; as shown in photograph 4 where I am unsuspectingly looking up in just the right direction at just the right time when Katie just happened to photograph orbs. Was it coincidence?

Over all, our experience included more instances of apparent purpose on the part of the luminosities than would seem likely by random chance.

One evening outside, we had the luminosities lined up as though posed for the photograph. (Photo. 31.) Again, coincidence?

When we first began to photograph orbs and we were still not sure if it was a lighting or lens effect; we said to ourselves that if only we had photos of orbs behind things that would be something. And we did: as already mentioned in Chapter 5 and as shown in photographs 3, 21 and 22.

As mentioned in Chapter 3 we wondered if the cats could see the luminosities, and we started to get shots of the cats looking as though they saw something as shown in photographs 13, 14 and 15. Again, was it coincidence? We don't think so. Sometimes it seemed as if the orbs were playing hide and seek with us, popping up here and there almost playfully. (Photos 32. & 33.)

Just check out photo 6 again. An orb is sitting next to the clock and there's another one between two wall plaques. Were they mimicking our ornaments? If they were humans one would suspect a sense of humour in some of these examples!

In common with most people of a creative turn of mind, when we photograph anything we unconsciously frame the image with an eye to composition. Though as far as orbs go, mostly we are shooting blindly, yet the luminosities consistently appear, more often than not, in the centre of the image, as though deliberately posed for a photo opportunity. Sometimes we got the definite impression that they wanted to be photographed! (Photos 34. & 35.)

Of course we are not the only people to have seen and

photographed luminosities. Whilst writing this book we had occasion to speak with various people and examine their own experiences of strange and mysterious luminosities.

STRANGE APPEARANCES OF LUMINOSITIES

One such incident is that of two friends who, a few years ago, were having dinner in their home one evening when they were surprised to see a ball of light suddenly appear and swirl through the air over the table and out through the patio doors.

They were amazed by the experience but had no idea why it occurred.

A woman in Yorkshire related the tale of how once from her bedroom window she had watched in fascination what she described as a dancing flame over the doorknob of the house directly opposite across the street. Again she had no idea what it was.

But luminosities are not only seen as one-off events, sometimes they are a recurring phenomena, their appearances often being associated with certain places.

We discovered that at one time, luminosities were such a widespread phenomenon, that virtually every county in the British Isles had its own name in the local vernacular for strange recurring light phenomena that had become part of local history.

For example: in South Yorkshire, these luminosities were called: 'Peggy wi't lantern', and in Wales; 'corpse candles'; and though not in current usage; the names; 'Will-o-the-wisp' and 'Jack-o-lantern', were once commonly used in 19th-century Britain to describe such odd luminosities. In other countries, this phenomenon also has a history, and is described by similar old local names; in Germany luminosities are known as 'Irrlichtern', meaning wandering light, and in

Sweden as; 'Lyktgubbe', meaning lantern bearer. In 1907 someone even photographed one floating through the Zoological Gardens in Basle, Switzerland. (Photo 36M.)

36M

Quite naturally attempts were made to explain these strange lights in terms of marsh gas, pockets of methane or phosphoresced hydrogen, which scientists speculated, could perhaps give rise to spontaneous luminescence. Although the chief failing of this explanation seems to be that phosphorous is never actually found in its pure state in nature, and laboratory tests so far have only been able to detect insignificant amounts of phosphorous in marsh gas anyway. According to all the available evidence it would seem that under natural circumstances the marsh gas theory is not very convincing. Though scientists assure us that possibly the natural occurrence of some as yet unknown self illuminating bio-gas could still be discovered to account for these cases of rather unscientific and perplexing luminosities.

The more we looked at instances of ball lightning and other luminosities the more we felt that there was a connection here with what we were experiencing. And it seemed fairly reasonable at the time to assume that both orbs and ball lightning were plasma concentrations. But even if this was so, it still did not explain the many accounts of witnesses who down through the years had reported ball lightning and luminosities performing complex movements; dancing or leaping over hedges, ascending high into the air or moving against the prevailing wind. Even more interestingly, over the years luminosities had often been reported as either moving away from someone who approaches them or following a person who is retreating from them.

The luminosities seemed to evidence intent; as the following cases illustrate.

Early last century, two Lake District Fell walkers, returning across country to Keswick, passed by Castlerigg stone circle just in time to see a collection of white luminous spheres floating around above the circle. As they watched this amazing display, one of the lights detached from the others and approached them. Before reaching them it just winked out as though whatever held it together had suddenly run out of energy.

In his book Uninvited Visitors, Ivan T. Sanderson tells of a similar incident.

During the Second World War a contingent of British troops, stationed on the Island of Curacao, were marching at night along the road that led to their billets around an oil refinery they had been sent to protect. Suddenly, out of the sky descended a sphere of luminescent peacock green light, about two feet in diameter. Landing in front of the men, it seemed to bounce along the road before them. Only momentarily fazed, the officer quickly ordered some men to catch it, but the sphere easily evaded them and shot off the road into a culvert. Troops were then deployed to either end of the culvert; with one party sent to enter by the open end. Unfortunately they were too slow. The luminosity easily evaded them, rose silently into the sky and vanished.

During the Second World War, Foo Fighters were a mysteriously common occurrence. And though Foo Fighters have often been associated with UFOs, it seems possible that some of these reports may in fact be of luminosities, similar to ball lightning. They also appeared during the Korean and Vietnam wars; and in all these aerial conflicts, Foo Fighters have been consistently reported by men on both sides; by both fighter pilots and bomber crews. British, American, German and Japanese pilots were equally plagued by this phenomenon.

Foo Fighters were also known as Foo Balls, Kraut Fireballs or Fireball Fighters, descriptive terms which seem to echo the appearance of ball lightning. They have been variously described as glowing balls or spheres, sometimes as discs but these do not account for the majority, mostly they are ball-like and any where from 12 inches to a few feet in diameter and usually orange or white in colour.

They were named Foo Fighters after a pun in a comic strip popular at the time called, 'Smokey Stover'. In this cartoon the French word "feu" (fire) was translated as, "where there's foo, there's fire". Foo Fighters were not detected by radar and attempts by pilots to out-manoeuvre these luminosities usually proved useless. Usually flying in formation, the Foo Balls tagged bomber squadrons and fighter planes. Often they would accompany single aircraft back to base. Sometimes they would approach aircraft at speed, circle or pace it and then fly away. Apart from the idea of UFOs there has never been any satisfactory explanation of Foo Fighters. Whilst not discounting the validity of the theory of UFOs as intelligently controlled craft of unknown purpose; it is interesting to note that the reported appearance and behaviour of some UFOs is consistent with the concept of large electrically propelled plasma concentrations, such as ball lightening.

Some while ago I had the opportunity to speak with a man who had been a test pilot. I asked him if he'd ever seen a UFO. He neatly sidestepped the subject by saying that the strangest thing he'd ever seen was when he was test flying a new aeroplane.

The whole fuselage was stripped down and contained only the

necessary instruments. Along with two engineers and another pilot he was busy at his tasks when suddenly a luminous ball of blue light about the size of a beach ball entered the plane through the hull near to the tail. To the total amazement of the crew it glided up and down the interior for a few minutes, then retracing its course exited the plane near to where it had entered. He had no idea what it could have been.

Another example of a strange luminosity getting too close for comfort; is the case of Mr Terry Pell who, very early one morning, whilst driving his lorry towards Warminster in Wiltshire, England; saw a large ball of light which moved towards him and fastened itself onto his windscreen. As he brought the vehicle to a sudden stop, his passengers, his wife and daughter woke up to see the luminosity ascending into the sky. This incident is faithfully documented in Arthur Shuttlewood's book, The Warminster Mystery.

Luminosities such as: orbs, spheres and flying balls of light are all phenomena often reported by UFO investigators. Indeed as well as appearing as the famous 'Foo Fighters' reported by 2nd World War pilots, sphere-like luminosities have also been described by UFO investigators, witnesses and Abductees alike.

Tony Dodd, the well known UFO investigator; affirms that many of his own encounters with mysterious balls of light left him in little doubt that they were intelligent, or intelligently controlled. He told us of one occasion, on the Yorkshire moors at night. when a large orange coloured ball of light glided about 30 feet above his head. As it passed, he tried to send out his thoughts to it; asking it to acknowledge his presence. Whereupon it immediately stopped in mid air, blinked out for about 3 seconds and then reappeared. Taking this as a response, Tony then thought the question: 'Who are you?'

Instantly a message popped into his head: 'I am the father of fathers and you are the son of sons!' The object then glided away into the night; leaving Tony to ponder on the meaning of this rather intriguing reply.

Another account concerning balls of orange coloured light, but this time a lot smaller; is one related to us by two friends who were travelling in their car along a lonely highland road, one February evening in 1997 at around eleven pm; when suddenly an orange ball about the size of a grapefruit flew towards them, shot past the passenger side of the car and disappeared down the road the way they had just come. Moments later, it or another one came up from behind, flew alongside the driver and shot off into the distance. They could hardly believe their eyes, but they were even more startled when another orange ball came hurtling out of the dark towards them, shot over the roof of the car and vanished into the night. They said that in retrospect they both felt as though the orange balls were checking them out for some unknown reason. But if so the rest of their journey that evening was uneventful.

There are many reports which indicate that luminosities often evidence curiosity such as moving about in a deliberate and exploratory manner. Sometimes they are reported as having a distinctive sulphuric odour. When officially reported they are often categorised as a UFO or some form of ball lightning. But in the latter instance, contrary to the known physical laws governing lightning behaviour, these mysterious spheres often totally ignore lightning rods and grounded conductors. As we looked through more reports we had to ask ourselves; would balls of plasma really behave like this? From what we'd learnt so far, the plasma theory certainly didn't account for everything that was reported about ball lightning. Although at the time it still seemed to me that there had to be something in the idea that ball lightning and orbs were both plasma concentrations of some kind. But even though it seemed a likely explanation for the physics of the thing, it fell a long way short of explaining the responsive, interactive, aspect of the phenomena.

One summer's day Katie and I sat out on the veranda and talked it over. Katie wasn't convinced that plasma theory alone had all the answers. I had to agree. It certainly didn't explain the incidences of apparent deliberate behaviour.

That didn't fit the theory at all. But it still seemed to me to be the best guess we had so far that fitted the physical properties of the luminosities.

That evening we drove out to a local high point and watched the sun go down. It was a dramatic sunset, with shades of vermilion, purple, bronze and golden yellows brushed across the sky. We watched as myriad hues of light touched the contours of lenticular cloud formations – all painted by light that had travelled 93 million miles in just about eight minutes to create yet another unique work of art in the atmosphere of Earth. No wonder the painter Turner had been so inspired to try and recapture something of the wonder of light. As we sat there we thought again about our own particular light phenomena.

Putting our own experience in the context of what we now knew of the whole luminosity phenomena in general there seemed to be two basic similarities; as far as behaviour went.

ONE: ball lightning, orbs and other related luminosities all displayed characteristics in the visible light spectrum suggesting electron-driven plasma concentrations. Interestingly, the reddish-orange and bluish-white colours often associated to UFOs and ball lightning, are the characteristic colours of ionised oxygen and nitrogen, the basic elements of air! Just the kind of effect plasma energy would produce.

TWO: luminosities have often been reported by witnesses to display controlled or intentional behaviour, added to which over the years there have been many independent reports of all these luminosities appearing, at times, to react intentionally with reference to the observer's movements, many witnesses being left with the impression that they may even react to their emotional states. Because of this it has been difficult for some people to avoid thinking of these luminosities as some kind of conscious entities.

We now had two possibilities; plasma energy and luminosities with consciousness. Of course, from a sceptical point of view, the latter raises the question as to whether witnesses may have superimposed their own preconceptions of intelligent behaviour onto the phenomena. We all have our own preconceptions about all kinds of things, and it is all too easy for sceptics, who were not there at the time, to trot this out as the only factual explanation, when in effect it is an opinion derived from their own preconceptions. But what particularly concerned us was not what the sceptics thought of it all but the question of whether plasma energies and consciousness were mutually exclusive?

At first I'd seen the plasma notion as contradictory to the behavioural aspect of luminosities but as Katie pointed out, the plasma idea didn't rule out any psychic or conscious element to the phenomena at all. It just explained it in physical terms. Human beings, for instance; are mostly fluid but we are still conscious entities, not just biological machines. So, it wasn't impossible that plasma concentrations could be merely the physical aspect, or signature at our level of reality, of a non-material life form. After all, we had now discovered that even on Earth certain types of bacterial life could exist inside volcanoes, in boiling springs and at sub-zero temperatures. At the beginning of the new millennium we are all learning that, life, is not bound by our old knowledge or perceptions.

The universe that is becoming visible to the world of 21st-century scientific enquiry is full of paradoxes and puzzling phenomena. It is a quantum universe, where for example; you can never catch an electron! The more you know of its speed, the less you know of its position, and vice versa. Nothing is as certain as it was in the world of Newtonian physics. Mysteries and probabilities abound in every sub-atomic nook and cranny. So why should it not, at least, be theoretically possible for our luminosities to be both plasma concentrations, and alive!

Looking at the sunset that evening, something else occurred to me. The clouds, though different in shape from each other, were not so different as to be mistaken for anything other than clouds. They all shared common physical factors that caused them to behave and appear the way clouds do. The fact that all the luminosities we had seen; photographed and researched, though individually different in size and colour; were all circular or spherical in construction, must mean that they all shared some common principle, which allowed them to be visible in those forms. And as we had discovered; circular and spherical forms had meaningful significance across the whole spectrum of belief and symbolism.

Reports of all kinds of luminosities were common throughout history and many of them were collected and documented last millennium by Charles Fort; who was a collector of all kinds of odd, curious and inexplicable facts. After his death in 1932, his work was practically forgotten until a small group of enthusiasts formed the 'Fortean Society.' Fort never committed himself to any single explanation for all the extraordinary phenomena and events he collected together, rather his position was more like sitting on the fence with both his ears to the ground, an accomplishment which defies most normal human limitations.

If we strip much of the light phenomena, logged by Fort, and others, down to its bare essentials, there are many similarities, exclusive of individual contexts, that implies that there is some common principal at work behind it all.

In spite of the paranormal aspect of our luminosities, they also seemed to be connected to the ordinary everyday world and to themes and symbols familiar to most of us. We were now convinced that just for them to be visible at all, meant there was a common physical mechanism at work in orbs and other luminosities. And all things considered, I still felt pretty sure that the plasma idea would prove to be correct, at least as far as the physics of the phenomena went. However, as is often the case, confidence is the feeling you get before you really understand the problem!

A few days later we had an electric storm and in a few short hours all my previous ideas on the nature of our luminosities were suddenly blown away! Out of the photographs that we took after the storm was one that stood out as being significantly different to any we had ever taken before.

Critical Angles:

Question: Does the notion of plasma concentrations seem to describe the physical properties of luminosities?

Answer: Yes.

Question: Is the apparent deliberate and purposeful behaviour of lumi-nosities explainable in terms of a non-conscious plasma energy form?

Answer: No.

CHAPTER 11

PHOTOGRAPHING FAIRIES

Such a soft floating witchery of sound,
As twilight elfins make, when they at eve,
Voyage on gentle gales from fairyland.

S.T. COLERIDGE

"And in the glade a light was seen of stars in shadow shimmering."

J.R.R. TOLKIEN, The Lord of the Rings

Ever since the day we had first photographed two orbs over the stream, we had been photographing them regularly throughout the garden. Big ones, small ones, singularly and in groups, with people, with cats; some static images and some with motion blur. We now had quite an interesting collection of images of these mysterious luminosities. Which we'd not only photographed, but at times had also seen as briefly visible twinkling lights. At this point we both believed that what we had seen and photographed was the whole of the phenomena; but we couldn't have been further from the truth! The first revelation of this was the unexpected image that appeared on one of the photographs we took after the electric storm. Here was something quite different to any other luminosity we had photographed before.

The new image was something neither of us had expected to see! (Photo. 36.)

One of the photographs we had taken the evening after the storm showed Katie and a few orbs beneath the trees, but also present was something else. Next to her, but slightly in the foreground, is what appears to be a hovering winged form of some kind. It was an amazing image but we had no idea what it was. All we knew was that for the first time we had photographed something that definitely wasn't an orb.

But it was thought provoking. This image suggested something else. When we enlarged it, we saw that indeed it clearly appeared to be a winged apparition. We stared at it in almost total disbelief. See enlargement (Photo. 36A.)

This was both incredible and intriguing, but it was also slightly disturbing. We had never photographed anything like it before, but there was little doubt as we studied it that it was disturbingly familiar. The implication seemed too impossible but as I looked at this strange image I could almost feel plasma concentrations dissolving into fairy dust. Katie and I looked at each other. It couldn't be – could it?

We enlarged it, we rotated it – it still looked unnervingly similar to something we had briefly glimpsed accidentally some years ago. Glimpsed but never photographed. Something which until now; we had both almost forgotten about. My mind did a quick mental rewind to one morning five years before.

WHAT WE SAW THROUGH THE WINDOW

That morning, after Katie had gone off to work early, I'd decided to follow in the footsteps of Hobbits and have a second breakfast. Sitting in the front room with a hot drink and some toast, I noticed Oscar, our ginger cat, making his way across the lawn. Was he stalking something? Suddenly he stopped and looked up. Something flittered out of the trees at the edge of the grass. Something that looked very odd. Jumping up I got to the window just in time to see it disappear over the hedge and across the stream into the woodland.

It happened so unexpectedly and so quickly that I hardly had time to mentally digest what I'd seen. What I'd seen was a white thing with wings. It was about the size of a chaffinch but it flittered like a butterfly. And it could easily have been a butterfly except for its size and for the fact that it had seemed to have a whitish hazy appearance, like something made of gauze or thick mist. Later I made a quick sketch to show Katie when she got home. (Figure. G)

Fig. G

Katie immediately thought it looked like either a moth or a Faerie. Which was probably right, but then it was only a drawing and I'd only seen it for a few moments. It was probably nothing, just a trick of the light. If it was something at all, it was in all probability a large tropical butterfly that had escaped from somewhere. I certainly wasn't inclined towards believing in cute little fairies with daffodil hats that sat around on toadstools. I stuck the sketch in a drawer and dismissed it from my mind, and the memory of it faded. Then one day, a couple of months later, again in the early morning, Katie and I were sitting together having breakfast in the front room when suddenly it, or something very similar, appeared again. This time we both saw it and leapt towards the window as it flittered out from the shrubbery, across the stream and away over the drive into the woodland at the edge of the fields. It all happened so quickly that there was no time to get a camera. Subsequently over the next two years we both saw the same thing, or some near relative to it, two more times; once in the same area of the garden and at about the same time of morning; and once around midday. But we never managed to be in time to photograph it. Realistically, my lost tropical butterfly explanation was now untenable; unless tropical butterflies are white, long lived, and can survive an English winter.

Still, people do see odd things, and as, after the last time, it never recurred, we did what most busy people do; stuck it in the mental filing cabinet and basically forgot about it. We never saw anything like it again, until we looked at the image before us on the computer. It did seem disturbingly coincidental; too coincidental perhaps?

We looked at it again. It was definitely not a bird or a bat. There were no birds out at night and we were well aware of bats flittering around, and of what they looked like,

We'd certainly never mistake one for anything else. The thing we had taken looked nothing like any normal kind of flying creature one would expect to accidentally photograph in the garden at night. And put together with the strange thing we'd seen flittering through the garden years before, our odd winged image did seem to suggest the impossible. Luminosities were one thing but 'faeries' in the garden – that was completely stretching the realms of probability!

The next evening, now spurred on by the idea that there may be something other than orbs about, we sallied forth to take some shots in the little dell; a place which Katie had always referred to as 'the Faerie Dell'. This may now sound like a rather all too apt name for it – but she had called it that ever since she first saw it; long before we saw anything odd or started photographing orbs. The Faerie Dell, as previously mentioned, is just next to the stream. The ash tree in the centre of the dell had obviously been planted within the moss-covered remains of a previous tree, possibly also an ash; as is often the custom of people who love trees. And the ring of medicinal plants around it had been put there by some long forgotten gardener. We often wondered who he or she was, and if they too had ever seen strange luminosities flitting through the shrubbery or accompanying them on walks through the woods.

In March the circle around the ash tree in the Faerie Dell is covered in bright yellow daffodils. The dell definitely has an enchanting quality all of its own; certainly our cats seem to like that particular area. Perhaps as the Dell is so close to the stream, the ions have a good effect on anyone in there? In any event the little dell has always felt a particularly wholesome place; if feelings are anything to go by. In the Faerie Dell we had photographed quite a few orbs and it was a place where we could usually count on getting a few good photographs, even if the elusive orbs had not popped up anywhere else in the garden.

After photographing the strange faerie-like image, Katie was so enthusiastic and optimistic that I too couldn't help but also feel a sense of expectation about our chances of seeing another winged entity in the garden. And almost as if the whole thing, as in Midsummer Nights Dream, had been prearranged by Oberon; that's exactly what hap-

pened! That same evening Katie took our second photograph of a winged form. This time quite appropriately, in the Faerie Dell. (Photo. 37.)

Like many of our orb shots this one was taken at dusk. Spurred on by success, Katie was now keener than ever for us to get out into the garden and woodland at twilight to try our luck. For it certainly seemed that the same principle that had applied to photographing orbs in the garden (as in: we'd hadn't photographed a single orb in the garden until the first two appeared over the stream and after that we got them all over the place) now also applied to photographing Faeries! Though initially not wishing to tempt fate too much we had simply called them, "winged things", which seemed fairly descriptive of the phenomena.

When out with our cameras at night we would usually follow the same route through the garden, first crossing over the little wooden bridge and then first stop the Faerie Dell. From there we would wander through the fringes of the woodland; cross over the stream again at the second little bridge by the wild cherry, follow the stream to the foot of the garden and then return home back along the drive.

As far as our Faerie-like images went, we did not initially rule out natural causes but after eliminating birds and bats as the culprits we wondered if there could be any other ordinary cause for our winged images. The last possibility in this area seemed to be moths.

To satisfy our curiosity on this we now tried to deliberately photograph moths – this wasn't easy and when we did get the odd one they looked nothing like what was on photograph 36. They looked just like what they were, distinctly moths. But don't just take our word for it – try it out – you'll find that there is a distinct difference between shots of natural phenomena, such as pollen, rain, insects, birds, bats, moths, etc and any images you may take yourself of genuine luminosities or winged things.

For we do not believe that any of this is unique to us, this phenomena is everywhere.

But it was the appearance of the faerie-like winged things that first made us realise that we may be dealing with an evolving phenomena, which though distinctly different to the orbs that we had first encountered may nevertheless be an extension or more complex form of luminosity. This seemed a reasonable assumption, especially as after we had photographed our first winged thing we were soon regularly photographing images of the faerie-like forms and often in company of our old familiar orbs.

And now when Katie chanced to see one or two of her lights and we took shots in that direction, as well as the luminosities we would sometimes also get the faerie-like phenomenon as well. Confirming that both luminosities and our "winged things" were probably connected to visible transient lights (STLs) in some way.

Trying to tune in to STLs, for anyone who does not naturally see them, is a bit like trying to make sense of one of those graphic images

38

that you have to put your eyes out of focus in order to see. You have to look in a different way, almost not look at all; like trying to see beyond or between the three dimensional world in front of us.

Though once you have the knack, and this will vary from individual to individual, you'll find that you'll see STLs more frequently.

However photographs taken of STLs can sometimes yield odd results, one image for example, where we'd both glimpsed a brief sparkle shows a dancing light in just about the same place. It wasn't a winged form, but it wasn't an orb either. (Photo. 38.)

One of my Pentax photo-graphs, taken the same night, shows a

39 .

winged light positioned neatly over Katie's head while she's crouched on the second little bridge about to take a shot. (Photo. 39.)

Some of the faerie-like images seemed to have been caught in the act of moving rapidly and some seemed to be in the process of form-shifting; as with one image we took late one

afternoon as we strolled along the woodland path. (Photo. 40.)

Was it an orb, a 'faerie' or something else?

Whatever it is, it appears to be travelling at speed. Even so it successfully got itself in the picture. In fact this, though travelling horizontally, was not the first luminosity we had photographed outside with what appears to be a movement trail or motion blur. One example of this showed many diverse individual elements that appeared to be moving. (Photo. 41.)

Could these have been luminosities transforming into the faerie-like forms?

As we photographed more winged things there was obviously a definite connection between them and our usual orbs. Often we had both together on one photograph.

Again, like the orbs, the faerie-like forms seemed at times to be mischievously aware of photo opportunities. Like orbs they also often appeared near to people and seemed to be brightest in proximity to living beings.

Photo. 42. shows both an orb and two winged things above Katie.

The more shots we took, the more we became convinced that the faerie-like forms were the same phenomena as the orbs, just configured differently. The faerie-like forms seemed to fit with our luminosities, but they were totally at odds with the idea of orbs and luminosities as plasma concentrations.

For most of us brought up within the current scientific perspective, time travel, other dimensions and aliens usually seem a whole lot more credible than old fashioned faeries and sprites. These entities are usually seen as denizens of fantasy and children's stories, or to a worldview long ago discredited by scientific rationalism.

We fleetingly wondered if perhaps in view of this we should keep quiet about the faerie angle. In the 21st century people who say they saw faeries at the bottom of the garden are often viewed with suspicion; as cranks or hoaxers. Even so we couldn't deny what we had seen and photographed, no matter how inconvenient it may be in terms of our credibility. Though we still had no clear idea of exactly what it was we were photographing. As we reflected on the whole thing, two main factors seemed to connect luminosities and faerie-like forms:

ONE: that we could actually photograph all three consistently; and:

TWO: that the Small Transient Light Phenomenon, was relevant to both phenomena. There was obviously a connection here. But what was it?

As we researched various material that may offer clues or

possibilities, we came upon the view, expressed by some writers on the subject, that UFO phenomenon and its associated entities had similarities with old tales of the activities of elves and faerie folk. Certainly there did seem to be some parallels with UFO entities and old accounts of encounters with faeries, especially in terms of missing time and the malevolent aspects. Though as far as we knew we ourselves had never experienced any missing time and our phenomena had never displayed any kind of malevolence at all; just the reverse, it had always felt friendly and playful.

As far as we were concerned, we had no indication that our phenomena had any connection with UFOs or aliens whatsoever, but we did begin to wonder if there could after all be some gleam of truth behind the whole concept of an elemental world of sprites and faeries.

Critical Angles:

Question: Are the appearances of winged, faerie-like forms explicable in terms of the concept of plasma concentrations as applied to orbs and other luminosities?

Answer: No.

Question: Does the fact that both luminosities and faerie-like forms, though different from each other in structure, are sometimes visible as the same Transient Light Phenomenon suggest they are connected?

Answer: Yes.

CHAPTER 12

LITTLE PEOPLE AND THE CAT
IN THE WINDOW

"Do there exist many worlds, or is there but a single world?"

ALBERTUS MAGNUS, 13th century

"From fairies, and the tempters of the night, guard me, I beseech you."

SHAKESPEARE

Many and diverse are the reasons given for the widespread belief in faeries; they are thought to be fallen angels, spirits of the dead, elementals, other dimensional beings, memories of forgotten peoples; even un-baptised babies. The faerie realm has certainly inspired artists, such as Henry Fuseli, who strikingly depicted Shakespeare's Oberon and Titania in the 1760s; and the Victorian painter Richard Dadd, who spent much of his life locked up in Bedlam, where he painted his vision of the miniature world of faeries. His detailed painting of a fairy axe-man about to split a hazelnut is hung in the Tate Gallery in London.

In some stories, faeries made their homes under human hearths and the 19th-century illustrator, James Nasmyth, drew a well-known study of tiny wingless faeries gathered around a log fire. Traditionally the best times to see fairies are twilight and midnight when the moon is full, themes reflected in the works of another Victorian painter of fairies, Richard Doyle. And of course most people are familiar with the enchanting illustrations of faeries, sprites and goblins by the 19th-century illustrator, Arthur Rackham. And more recently the realm of Faerie has inspired a whole wealth of entertaining books such as Brian Froud's 'Pressed Fairy Book', and the imaginatively, evocative, artwork of such illustrators as Charles Vess.

However to some people faeries are more than subjects for imaginative art. Within today's New Age movement many take the idea of Faerie and its kindred realms of Angels and Elementals (nature spirits) quite seriously.

As previously mentioned, the creator of Sherlock Holmes; also took the idea of faeries seriously and it was through him that the case of the Cottingley Fairies came to public attention. Although it would seem that, Sir Arthur Conan Doyle, unlike his famous detectives, Holmes and Watson, didn't actually investigate the facts himself. He completely believed the account of the two girls without question and used slides of their fairy photographs in his lecture tours, as proof for his own belief in the existence of faeries. Elsie and Frances, the girls in question, claimed to have seen fairies, or something they interpreted as fairies, in Cottingley Glen – but did they really photograph them? The exact truth of the whole matter is still open to debate but in any event the Cottingley photographs certainly cannot be regarded as proof of the existence of fairies. Far too many question marks hang over the whole episode.

Even so, the whole idea of two young girls photographing faeries has a strong appeal, so much so that two motion pictures, inspired by the Cottingley fairies, were released within a couple of years of each other.

The first; and more fanciful; 'Photographing Fairies', in 1997 and then in 1998 the film; 'Fairy Tale', which was based loosely on the story of Elsie and Frances, and which had its British premiere in Bradford. But whatever the exact nature of the Cottingley Fairies, we still had our own phenomena to try and get some kind of perspective on.

Excluding the overly romantic Victorian ideas of fairies, and the popular 1940s, 'Flower Fairies' by Cicely Mary Barker; was it conceivable that something real actually lay behind the old tales and legends of faeries?

Could any of this, we wondered, throw even a glimmer of light on what we had seen and photographed here in the 21st century?

The majority of mythical and folklore depictions of faerie folk that have come down to us through the ages can, so historians tell us, usually be traced back to their most likely historical roots. Most nature sprites and faeries, for example; are usually seen as being derived from pre-Christian gods and goddesses or from pagan concepts of water or tree spirits.

In medieval times it was a commonly held belief that faeries were elementals: creatures made only of earth, air, fire or water. Medieval sorcerers devised complex rituals and spells for conjuring them up and making use of their powers. At one time throughout the whole of Europe, belief in faeries was accepted as being totally credible and commonplace. Many of the most popular traditions associated with faeries originated in Britain. Like Ireland, Britain was widely known in ages past for being a special magical land where faerie folk had once dwelt.

As we looked deeper into this subject, we found it very interesting that tales of faeries, in every century, speak of them as if they were already creatures of the past.

Almost as if they were indeed part of another, older world.

Some experts cite the tradition that iron protects against faeries as evidence that our belief in faeries was derived from the memory of the original natives of Britain; who were supposedly small and dark, and had only weapons of bronze or stone. Pre-historians generally believe that they were driven into the hills by the invading, iron wielding Celts. Eventually these indigenous Bronze Age inhabitants of the British Isles became a furtive, secret people hiding in hills and remote places until they finally died out, later to reappear in fireside tales transformed into the faerie folk of legend. Some of these notions may partly explain the historical belief in faeries, but not entirely.

We discovered that anecdotal tales of encounters with faerie-like beings still persist right up to the present day. One woman that we spoke with told us of an experience she'd had whilst on a bus journey through the countryside one summer. As the coach moved slowly behind a tractor, she looked out of the window and to her utter surprise, saw a little man no more than two foot tall standing by a stream in the field opposite. He was wearing a dark sleeveless jerkin and a black hat. For some unknown reason she said he reminded her of a 'Flour Grader'.

A man from the south of England told us the tale his aunt used to tell of the time when she was out walking down a country lane and came upon a gate into a field. Sitting on this gate was a little man about two or three feet tall. He was wearing a dark coat and a pointed hat. When she stopped in surprise to stare at him, the little man suddenly looked at her with an expression of total shock and then abruptly disappeared.

One evening in conversation with, June, an Irish woman who was a college lecturer in fashion design, she spoke of the time when as a young girl in Ireland, in the 1960s, she'd been to a dance with her first sweetheart. They were walking back home when they spied a haystack. As the night was warm they climbed up on top of it and made love. When she woke up it was a moonlit night and she could hear something rustling in the field below. It sounded like rice-crispies.

Creeping to the edge of the haystack she peered over to see a whole host of little dark figures dancing through the mown field. She was amazed but a little afraid. Waking her lover they quietly peeped over at the small beings running here and there in the field below. Her lover was terrified lest they were spotted and didn't want to look anymore, but June lay there until sleep took her. When they woke again it was day light and they both recalled exactly the same dream of the little dark figures in the moonlight. June was convinced it was no dream at all but something real.

Even C.S. Lewis, who wrote 'The Lion the Witch and the Wardrobe', recalled, as a child, seeing a strange gnome-like little being in his garden. Interestingly he also recalled one day, as a child playing in the garden, he and his brother seeing a bright luminosity hovering over their playthings! Many creative people, have at times had strange experiences that can only be termed other worldly.

And all tales of faerie encounters, whether ancient or modern have this other worldly quality to them – as though the experiencers were in some kind of enchanted dream spun by Puck. But why do they, people from all times and places, tell very similar tales and describe very similar beings? Little people with pointed hats are obviously drawn from human imagination, but what has fired that? What is it that lies buried in the human subconscious, which manifests through the creatures from the Realm of Faerie? We wondered if it was just possible that there was some aspect of Faerie Llore that could be relevant to our own experience and to the odd Faerie-like things we had been photographing.

Taking into account the usual theories and explanations for faeries, exotic and otherwise, there is one element that is fundamental to all tales and legends of faeries everywhere; and that is, the universal belief that faeries come from another world. A world that is seen as being: betwixt and between here and somewhere else.

This otherworldly aspect is obviously very meaningful in terms of the human subconscious because it has been so widely externalised in our popular conceptions of faeries, and underpins the elaborate constructions of most fictional fantasy.

Faeries are archetypical creatures. Jung believed that the fairy tales and myths of the world contained archetypes, creatures and themes that recur again and again in the fantasies, dreams and delusions of the human mind. We are subconsciously impelled towards certain archetypes. Perhaps this accounts for the incredible enduring popularity of Tolkien's The Lord of the Rings. Some enthusiasts even go so far as to believe that at one level the history of Middle-earth is actually real, or that it feels more real than actual history. Perhaps this is because it speaks directly to the primeval attraction to archetypes buried deep inside the human mind?

Jung may have been the 'father of archetypes' but it is a fact that more people are familiar with the works of Tolkien than they are with the works of Jung. Such is the power of archetypes!

Whether you actually believe in the Faerie Realm or not, humans throughout history and in every country have been impelled, for whatever reasons, to conceive of certain events in the phenomenal world around them as being of 'otherworldly' origin.

As we researched this we began to see possible similarities to our own phenomena.

It has been said of faeries that they can appear in the twinkling of an eye, and disappear in the same manner. Both Transient Lights and luminosities do this.

It is inherently the nature of faeries to be elusive, not conforming to the usual physical laws by which we are bound, a facility they share in common with orbs and luminosities.

Of particular interest to us was the fact that faeries are often associated with lights and luminosities; and known by various names, such as Jack O'Lantern, Will o' the wisp, Spunkie, Pinket and Ignis Fatuus, a term meaning foolish flame.

Interestingly, most of the parochial terms for faeries were also applicable to, and interchangeable with, the phenomenon of fire balls, ghost lights, and anomalous luminosities in general.

Some of the faerie light phenomenon was reputedly mischievous, often leading people into bogs, or causing them to lose their way. Sometimes strange light phenomenon, when associated to faeries, evidenced a shape-shifting aspect, reputedly disguising itself as a beautiful young maiden or a crock of silver to lead the unwary traveller astray. Our own phenomenon, hadn't so far resorted to anything as exotically devious but the transition of the phenomena, at times, from orb-like luminosities to winged faerie-like apparitions did seem, in a small way, to echo the shape-shifting abilities of the faeries of legend.

Most fairy tales have, of course, been distorted by time, by cultural influence and by deliberate censorship, such as by the church or state or even by parental control. The traditional fairytale Elves and Fairies are obviously highly romanticised characters derived from popular misconceptions of older myths and legends.

But no doubt at some point in the distant past even myths had some basis in fact.

As we strolled through the woodlands one day, with thoughts of faeries and ancient legends still fresh in our minds, we stopped in front of an old oak tree. Its massive structure tall and impressive with twisted trunk and branches so set out that it strikingly recalled one of the Ents of Fangorn Forest in The Lord of the Rings.

We now noticed that we were actually standing in the middle of a circle of old trees. All bent and twisted, rather unnervingly, in almost human-like postures, just as though we had interrupted a meeting of old and hoary woodland gods. As the afternoon sunlight slanted through the trees, it was easy to see how early peoples had believed in woodland elves and spirits of the forest. Was it our imagination – or was there something else there, an animating spirit, hidden behind tree and leaf? Almost instinctively we touched the bark of the old oak. The many fingered branches creaked and a myriad leaves whispered. Almost we could feel what it meant to be a tree. Rooted in the Earth but touching heaven; the feeling of a slow unhurried awareness stretching backwards into the past and forwards into the future. As skin touched bark we could feel the presence of something. Or was it just imagination?

In the old glade the original substance of myth and archetype still engaged both human eye and emotions just as they must have done ten thousand years ago.

Small wonder that it was easy to believe in the Ents of Middle-earth, or in the mythic dryads and nymphs frolicking in the woods of Europe long ago. We could imagine how ancient people, who sensed much more of the living Earth around them than we do, could perhaps feel the elemental forces of water, wood and wind that are unseen by the physical senses. Could this otherworldly concept of faeries that was buried in the human psyche, be a metaphor for something else? Some other reality maybe, or some primal elemental force? Electromagnetism? Chi energy? Could this something Other, be what Indians called, the Great Spirit? Something which responds to or interacts with human consciousness?

Later, as I thought more about the possible similarities of faeries, sprites and luminosities, I recalled that one of my old lecturers, a straight forward down to earth Irish man, had taken the idea of 'faerie folk' quite seriously, claiming to have once seen them crossing a road one moonlit night. But whether or not this was literally true, anthropomorphic little people didn't seem to fit with our luminosities.

Our phenomena didn't leave footprints. Even the faerie-like forms, though not explicable as balls of plasma, still evidenced the characteristics of a non-material energy based phenomena. If they were conscious entities then they were of a much different order to humans; and to the rather trite idea of small bipeds with wings.

If the luminosities and faerie-like forms, were beings at all, then they existed in the realm of light and energy. And whatever we believed about the likelihood of faeries in our garden, the fact was that, whether we liked it or not, we were now photographing something that looked suspiciously faerie-like.

Behind our two dimensional images there seemed to be something else at work.

So far our experience of this phenomena had undoubtedly been a positive one, and it had always felt friendly, yet we still had no real idea what it was – or what it all meant, if anything.

Colour originals of previous black and white photographs.

Photo: 7. Room full of orbs.

Photo: 15. Orbs and Oscar.

Photo: 35. Orange luminosity

Photo: 36. First winged form.

Colour originals of previous black and white photographs.

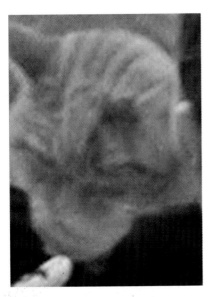

Photo: 43A. Image enlargement.

Photo: 45. Spherical luminosity.

Photo: 46D. Light rod.

Photo: 49A. Constellation.

Colour originals of previous black and white photographs.

Photo: 57. Light being.

Colour originals of previous black and white photographs.

Photo: 62. Water ceremony apparition.

Colour originals of previous black and white photographs.

Photo: CP1. Woodland walk, Spring 2004.

Additional colour photographs.

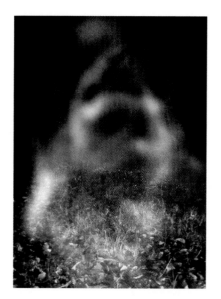

Photo: CP2. Dancing Light-forms.

Photo: CP3. Strange luminosity.

Photo: CP4. Curious cat.

Photo: CP5. Sky orbs.

Additional colour photographs.

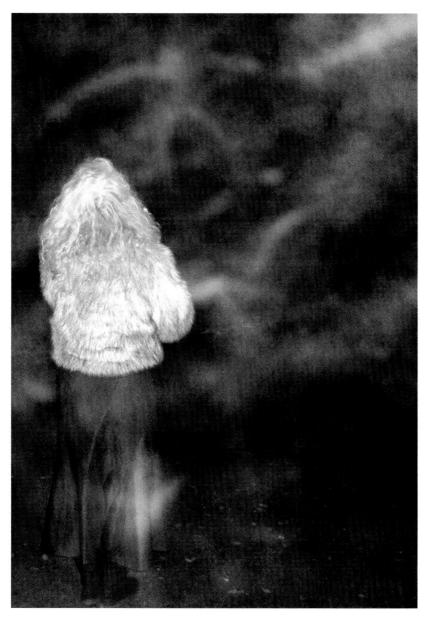

Photo: CP6. Ethereal Light-forms.

Additional colour photographs.

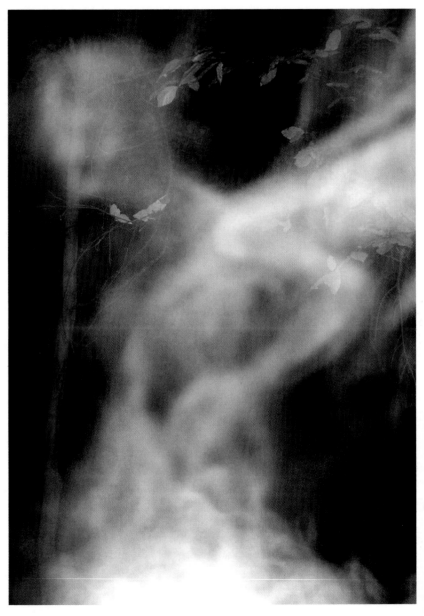

Photo: CP7. Winged apparition.

THE STRANGE IMAGE ON THE CAT
IN THE WINDOW

We were still pondering on all this when one afternoon, not long afterwards, a good friend turned up with her little boy. We'd known Ben since he'd been born, and although only one year old he was, as they say, 'a real smart cookie'. He was interested in everything, particularly the large 17th-century sea chest we had in the hall, which was full of various toys for visiting children. If he wanted toys to play with, Ben had learned to go into the hall and knock on the lid of the sea chest. His parents had already taught him some sign language and although he wasn't yet talking he could communicate with signs pretty well. That particular day, while we were all sitting around chatting, Ben was happily entertaining himself looking out of the floor length windows in the front room. He was watching our two cats, Baggy and Oscar, who were sitting out on the veranda. Ben had always been fascinated by the cats, and he was busily making the sign for 'cat' at them. Obviously this didn't impress the cats much as they already knew who they were. What they didn't know was why we weren't letting them in. Oscar, our ginger cat, came over and complained directly to little Ben. For a while cat and toddler faced each other at opposite sides of the window, one meowing, the other signing. It made a good photo opportunity. Fortunately I managed to get a shot before either of them moved away; as both cats and children are wont to do when you are all set to take a photograph.

We'd already taken a few shots that afternoon but as Ben and his Mum had to go, and we had to get some stuff in the post, we didn't look at them that day. A couple of days later when we looked at the shot of Ben and Oscar at the window, we realised that we'd captured something very odd. (Photo. 43.)

At first we'd thought it was an orb, but on closer examination this image of Ben and Oscar seemed eerily appropriate to our present preoccupation with faeries. If you study the enlargement below, (43a) you will perhaps see what we mean.

We've subsequently shown this image to quite a few people. At first some are not sure what they see. Some see a meaningless smudge, others a face, and some instantly see something else; the same thing that we both saw when we first looked at it. Once it's pointed out people often find it difficult to then see it as anything else. Again it's a bit like looking at one of those optical puzzle pictures. So it may help to hold the photograph about a foot away and squint at it. Hopefully you will now see the image of what looks like the top half of a girl with brown hair, bare arms and a white top; sitting with her knees up and head tilted down slightly, as though either looking down at her hands or at a book. But we must emphasise

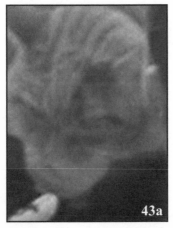

here that we do not consider this image as any kind of proof whatever for the actual existence of Flower Faeries or anything remotely similar! Still, in the context of our phenomena overall, it is certainly a curiously apt image.

Certainly at the time, considering our current interest in faerie phenomena, it did rather seem like somebody's idea of a joke. The image on Oscar's head, once seen, does look remarkably like the classical conception of a flower faerie. And it must be pointed out that little Ben definitely wasn't wearing a T-shirt with a printed fairy picture on the front. His T-shirt had only two colours, dark blue and light blue.

Once more, perplexingly, we had an odd image which certainly didn't fit in with our previous ideas, plasma or otherwise. Interestingly, friends who were inclined towards believing in the paranormal mostly saw it as a faerie straight away. Even a couple of our more sceptical friends admitted it looked like a girl reading. Though of course some people saw nothing of the kind, however the majority consensus seemed to be that the image was that of a girl. But who, and from where?

Could this really be a rather prosaic manifestation from the realm of faerie?

Neither Katie nor I seriously thought this a realistic possibility and we looked around for some other explanation.

Psychology seemed to have one on offer!

For years people have seen pictures in the clouds, or patterns on rocks, or mirages in deserts; images of all kinds; faces, animals and aliens. Even recently on Ebay someone sold a piece of burnt toast with the image of the Virgin Mary on it!

All these images can be put down to our human ability to make sense out of random elements – to anthropomorphise the world around us – seeing troll-like faces in knotted tree trunks or the face of Jesus in the facets of a beer glass. Some would say this is the most likely explanation, for our image, but even if that is true, it still did not explain the appearance of a faerie-like image at exactly the very time we were researching faeries relative to the faerie-like images now popping up on our photographs! Could it be coincidence? Well, maybe! But for us, in the light of our previous experience with the luminosities there seemed far too many instances of meaningful coincidences for it all to be merely the product of pure chance.

Winged images have echoes in the human psyche: they are symbols of freedom, aspiration, transcendence, rebirth, and ascension to a higher plain. Beneath all the visual phenomena, we now suspected that there was something else at work; something perhaps woven through, and underlying the world of our senses.

Critical Angles:

Question: Are there similarities between the non-anthropomorphic aspects of faerie phenomena, and the recorded behaviour of luminosities?

Answer: Yes.

Question: In the context of the transition of luminosities into winged faerie-like forms and our research into faerie legends; could the appearance of the rather prosaic classical faerie-like image in the window at that specific time be considered a synchronistic event?

Answer: Yes.

CHAPTER 13

SYNCHRONICITY

"The problem of synchronicity has puzzled me for a long time, ever since the middle twenties, when I was investigating the phenomena of the collective unconscious and kept on coming across connections which I simply could not explain as chance..."

C. G. JUNG, *Synchronicity: an Acausal Connecting Principle*

Reconciling the visible Small Transient Lights Phenomena with the idea of our luminosities as plasma concentrations had initially seemed to work reasonably well on most levels, but with the recent appearance of the faerie-like forms, the plasma theory no longer seemed a very likely explanation. We began to re-examine what we'd learned and experienced so far and there was one major factor that had been a consistent link through all levels of our phenomena, and that was the regular occurrence of meaningful coincidences. These coincidences seemed to occur with a relevance and frequency that made pure chance seem improbable. And it seemed likely that synchronicity was the connecting mechanism between the phenomena and our experience of it.

Accordingly we shall now take a look at synchronicity.

For many individuals with no particular paranormal axes to grind, one of the most convincing indicators that alongside our material world something else is happening, is the everyday occurrence of synchronicity in their lives. Synchronicity is the term coined by the famous psychologist C.G. Jung to designate: the meaningful coincidence, or equivalence, of psychic or physical states or events which are not directly related; or when an inwardly perceived insight, such as a dream, vision or premonition has direct meaning for external reality. The word can also be used to describe similar or identical thoughts or dreams occurring at the same time in different places. Jung described this as an 'Acausal Connecting Principle' and cited it as possible evidence for his hypothesis of the collective unconscious.

Though even he seemed to struggle at times to reconcile the inexplicable existence of synchronicity with the orthodox assumption of a purely relative mechanistic universe, pointing out that:

"meaningful coincidences are unthinkable as pure chance..."

Whatever interpretations we, who have come after Jung, may place on synchronicity; time, events and research have shown it to be a real phenomena by which meaningful coincidences are at work in our world. In fact so convinced of this was Jung that he kept a personal logbook of coincidences. A particularly interesting incident of synchronicity occurred while Jung was treating a young female patient in his rooms: on this particular afternoon the young woman had been describing a dream in which she was given a golden scarab. Jung, who had been sitting with his back to the window, heard a gentle tapping against the glass. Turning, he saw a flying insect knocking itself against the window-pane. When he opened the window it flew inside and he caught it in his hand. To his surprise he was holding the nearest creature to a golden scarab that could be found in Europe: a scarabaed beetle, usually known as the common rose-chafer. Totally contrary to its normal habits, for some unknown reason it had felt an urge to get into Jung's room just as his patient was recalling her dream about the scarab.

While Jung was investigating the phenomena of the collective unconscious he kept coming upon instances of coincidences time and time again, coincidences that were so meaningfully connected that, as Jung put it; " their 'chance' concurrence would represent a degree of improbability" so great that it would have to be "expressed by an astronomical figure."

To Jung, the incidence of coincidence seemed so wide spread throughout the world at all levels that this fact of itself negated the whole concept of chance coincidence.

Interestingly our literary agent, upon receiving the first draft of this book, experienced such an incidence of unlikely coincidence. Until reading our book she had known nothing of orbs and certainly had no previous cause at all to think about that word. Strangely, in the next few days the word 'orb', cropped up three times as either answers or clues in newspaper crossword puzzles.

Synchronistic events happen all the time to practically everyone, so much so that we take them for granted. When we first began this account one of our possible titles was Light Fantastic, but for some reason we rejected this and chose the current title.

This was just as well because, the very next week on TV there was a new programme about light, called Light Fantastic! You've probably noticed similar coincidences with films, like the two different film companies who both made films about Robin Hood, which were released within weeks of each other.

The same happened with two different films about Wyatt Earp, the children's film, Antz and its Disney counterpart, Bug's Life; and it has happened with numerous others. Almost as soon as you think up a really good idea, chances are that you are bound to see it done by somebody else. A friend of ours once spent two years writing a book on the Pre-Raphaelites. He had shown his book to no one until it was finished and he was happily on his way to post off his synopsis to a friend, when calling into his local bookshop, he was devastated to see that there on the shelf was a new book on the same subject, using the same title and practically the same treatment! Coincidence, or rather synchronicity, had struck again.

Of course not all synchronistic events are bad; fortunately it works both ways. Just when you're down to your last packet of crisps, a great aunt may suddenly leave you a fortune. Or you may go on holiday to some distant place only to find yourself sitting opposite your long lost childhood sweetheart at breakfast. Synchronicity is a common denominator in many people's lives.

Luminosities apart, for Katie and I, synchronicity has certainly played a part in our own relationship. When we first met it was by chance for no more than 20 minutes at a trade fair, after which we had no contact whatsoever for four years. During that time neither of us had any idea as to what the other was doing or even where they were, and we were completely unaware that the events in our individual lives and the decisions we were making, even the thoughts we were thinking, were actually drawing us together, to the point where one day we met, again by chance, on the street of a small market town, miles away from where either of us lived.

This time, fortuitously, everything in our own lives, and even in the lives of our families, was coincidentally conducive for us to be together. As often happens, when people respond to the synchronicity of events in their lives, positive changes often occur. Certainly from our own experience of synchronicity, our own lives and the lives of our family and friends have been enriched and expanded in ways that, we believe, could not have happened otherwise. Others could tell similar stories.

Even in terms of the luminosities, synchronicity was already at work in our lives even before we had taken our first photograph of an orb. If I was asked to pinpoint the beginning of our light phenomena, I would have to say that it really began a few years previously. It happened like this: the first week that I moved into Brackenbeck, it was February and I was more or less camping there, sleeping at night in the front room where I could keep warm by the fire. One morning I woke up just as it was getting light. At that time not only did I not have a bed; I had no furniture to speak of either. What I did have was a room full of boxes and three cats locked in the kitchen where they were temporary prisoners for the next week, until they got used to their new home. I opened the front door and stepped out for a breath of morning air. Just then a small herd of deer emerged out of the early morning mist, trooped slowly across the garden and disappeared into the woodland. I'd never seen wild deer so close before. It was an enchanting sight and immediately I wished that Katie, who I'd met the week before, could have been there to see them. Later that day, at around 4 o-clock, I was on my way to give the cats their tea; when entering the hall I came to a sudden stop. Floating in the air, approximately eight feet from the marble floor, was a cloud of tiny twinkling lights, each no bigger than a bird's eye, scintillating brightly in the dimness of the hall, like bonfire night sparklers. Hardly breathing, I watched the fantastic light display in total fascination. Within two or three minutes they gradually faded away, until at last they were gone. I had no idea what they were; but it was certainly an amazingly magical moment. Perhaps it was some kind of confirmation that maybe I was now in the right place.

Then four years later, one afternoon of the first week Katie moved in with me she too saw a swirling cloud of tiny sparkling lights, but this time, moving up and down near the ceiling in the front room; where we were later to photograph orbs. We compared notes and we couldn't help but wonder if they were the same ones that I'd seen four years earlier. And so our life together at Brackenbeck began with the synchronistic appearance of strange lights. We didn't know then what they were; or that a few years later we would be photographing orbs and other odd light phenomena.

At the time we simply took them as a positive sign for our new life together. This may sound overly romantic, but I guess it rather depends on how you view the world.

Some people believe life is a random process; things just happen by chance. When it comes to the crunch they are on their own, there's no reason to events – they're merely the result of chance or cause and effect. Others believe the very existence of consciousness itself implies purpose. For those people, events have meaning and whatever that may be; they don't believe that they face the world alone. Like threads in a tapestry they are part of a larger design. It depends upon which perspective you see as to how you interpret any given event, especially the more extraordinary ones.

Personally, all I know is that from my own experience, I don't believe that anything happens by chance; even though as individuals we may not know at the time all the connections. And now, I'm even more inclined towards the belief that at some level there is a fundamental connective principle at work in life.

What we have experienced here at Brackenbeck seems to confirm that woven through the whole of our phenomena is some kind of connecting thread. Connecting the lights we both first saw here, to the luminosities. Perhaps connecting those same luminosities to events: such as the night when a verbal comment resulted in a whole roomful of orbs? Perhaps too connecting both orbs and faerie-like forms to the visible Transient Lights!

All we had witnessed left us in little doubt that something else was at work behind the visual images. Like Jung, and many others, we have to affirm that synchronicity exists. We have seen synchronicity at work in our own lives, in the lives of others and, more pertinently to this book: in the behaviour of our mysterious luminosities.

Something more extraordinary than merely photographing orbs was happening.

If we think of Jung's view in which even the normal instance of coincidence is so ubiquitous that it makes nonsense out of the concept of coincidence itself; then we are left with the possibility of a fundamental process at work in the world: a process that implies an underlying connectivity of consciousness and meaning to events.

Like the realm of faeries, the concept of synchronicity could be said to be a betwixt and between place, rubbing shoulders with: mysticism, quantum physics and precognition, all of which infer the reality of synchronicity; and all of which have in common the ability to think the unthinkable. In the following pages we shall explore the possible connections there may be behind the luminosities and what may, or may not, prove unthinkable.

Critical Angles:

Question: Is the consistent occurrence of synchronicity relative to all levels of the phenomena suggestive of a connective principle at work?

Answer: Yes

Question: Does the synchronicity noted in the phenomena, such as the specific appearance of the faerie-like image in the window; and the general tendency of the phenomena to appear deliberately responsive, suggest the possibility of purpose?

Answer: Yes

CHAPTER 14

GHOST LIGHTS AND THE SUPERNATURAL

"How can we know the state of the dead, seeing we hardly know the state of the living?"

CONFUCIUS, 550-477 BC

"As Children tremble and fear everything in the blind darkness, so we in the light sometimes fear what is no more to be feared than the things children in the dark hold in terror..."

On The Nature of Things, LUCRETIUS, C.60 BC

We were now quite often photographing faerie-like forms as well the usual orbs, and after our initial shock at this kind of appearance we were now quite used to it.

And apart from our continued efforts to try and figure it out we had to all practical purposes accepted it as yet another puzzling manifestation of our phenomena at Brackenbeck. It was during the latter part of this time that Katie's brother Sam visited again for a weekend. For some reason, we can't think why, he was now getting interested in all kinds of areas he would previously never have considered, such as other dimensions, past life regression and meditation. Plus, he was now keen to see if we could photograph luminosities in a place traditionally associated with strange and spooky events: the graveyard.

From being a sceptic, Sam had now turned into an apprentice ghost hunter!

Fair to say, in all our deliberations, so far on the causes behind the luminosities, the supernatural was one area that we had not given much real consideration to. Perhaps it was time that we did. Obligingly, late that Saturday night, we took Sam with us to a lonely old country graveyard that wasn't too far away.

Silent, shadowed and mysterious in the dark the old graveyard certainly had all the right elements to work on the imagination. Except for the dead, the three of us were entirely alone. There were probably no other people for miles. Some may have thought it was just the setting that Dracula would choose for a picnic spot.

But we had been in similar places before at the dead of night and we had never yet felt any real sense of fear. Certainly not fear of the dead. In our experience it is usually the living that one needs to be more wary of, especially if they happen to be in charge of your country,

your future or your environment. By day this spot was a charming old country graveyard; and by night it was not much different, except for what the imagination of day dwelling bipeds; who can't see very far in the dark, could conjure up.

A hedgehog rustled along by the wall, not concerned with the doings of people, whether living or dead. We wandered about for a while and indeed did get a few shots of luminosities that night, but no faerie-like forms. (Photo. 44.)

These didn't seem particularly spooky to us, they were just the usual orbs.

Still, thanks to Sam's prompting, we did begin to look a bit closer at supernatural explanations for what we had encountered. Was it possible that the orbs we had photographed were actually spirit phenomena? Many people think that orbs, like vapours, vortices and apparitions fall into the category of spirit manifestations, by which they usually mean manifestations generated by the spirits of the dead.

We began to look into the area of the supernatural in relation to our phenomena and soon acquired two very interesting pieces of information that to us seemed particularly relevant to the question of orbs and spirits of the departed.

The first came from a man who had one night stood vigil by the grave of a recently departed loved one. As he recounted it; during that night, he saw many lights, like luminous spheres rising up from the nearby grave of a newly buried person. He felt no fear at this extraordinary sight, rather he felt comforted, believing them to be angels accompanying the spirit of the departed soul on its way to heaven.

This account was not too dissimilar to other reports we had read of luminosities or ghost lights associated with places where people had died.

In Derbyshire we met, Sylvia, a lady who, as a young woman working in a hospital, had been on her way back to her room in the nurses' quarters when she saw a bluish misty luminosity rising up in front of a door. Going with her intuition, she called the warden and they discovered a nurse who had tried to take her own life and who probably would have died, had it not been for that misty apparition.

There is little doubt that spirit phenomena exist, from white ladies, phantom animals and haunted houses to poltergeist activities, all of which have been well recorded. Many tales of ghosts and spirits includes strange light phenomena such as floating lights, columns of light, misty swirls of light and flickering flame-like effects. Often these are associated with tales of violent, sad or untimely deaths. In certain places, the regular appearances of translucent, misty forms, have given rise to the tales of many white or grey lady ghosts. One of the most famous of these kinds of apparitions is the Brown Lady of Raynham Hall in Norfolk. She is believed to be Dorothy Walpole, the sister of Robert Walpole, Britain's first Prime Minister. There are various macabre versions of her untimely death. Famous in the annals of ghost phenomena is the photograph of this Brown Lady, taken by two Country Life photographers who were staying at Raynham in the 1930s. This photograph has been frequently included in books about ghosts and actually shows not a Brown Lady, but a transparent, misty column of light on the stairs.

Take it out of the context of Raynham Hall, this misty apparition could easily be interchangeable with reports of other light phenomena, such as: Will O' the Wisp, ghost lights; and other luminous roaming vapours in general.

Columns of light and misty vapours appear in many places other than haunted houses. In the Midlands, we spoke with a farmer who was used to walking the lonely hills and moors at night. One particular winter's night, he was on his way down to the village. A light scattering of snow covered the moor-land path; it was a route he'd taken many times; he was about halfway to his destination when he had the strong feeling that he was not alone. Turning in his tracks, he found himself looking at a column of orange light floating over the path behind him. He stared at it in amazement. Within a few minutes it began to fade until it was gone. Pragmatically the farmer explained his experience like this: 'If I'd been a Roman Catholic, I'd have thought it was the Virgin Mary, If I'd been a spiritualist; probably a ghost; and if I'd believed in UFOs I'd have thought it some kind of alien. But as I don't believe in any of those things, it was just an orange light!' This is a refreshing way of looking at odd phenomena and perhaps we would all do well to remember that our preconceptions may sometimes completely obscure the real nature of what we are experiencing.

There are many tales of ghostly and supernatural experiences and though many of them are anecdotal, some are well witnessed. But it is not our business here to decide whether any of what people term spirit phenomena is actually true or not; only to determine if it is a viable explanation for our own luminosities.

Our second particularly relevant encounter was with, Gladis, an elderly woman who lived in Peckham. She had lived there during the Second World War and had lost both friends and relatives during that time. Gladis recalled many grieving wives, sisters and mothers visiting mediums in those days. Many found comfort there but later, some found that those they had thought dead had actually only been missing! Yet mediums had been successfully contacting them as departed souls; telling grieving relatives things that only they or the dead could possibly know. We had heard of similar experiences before, even though some of the mediums involved were reputable people with genuine psychic abilities.

This posed an interesting question: from where were the mediums getting their information? To all intents and purposes the mediums in these cases must have genuinely believed they were in contact with departed souls – but if that wasn't really the case, who, or what, were they in contact with?

Over the past few years the supernatural has become very popular, especially in terms of entertainment and the media; with an increasing proliferation of TV programs based around the subject of paranormal phenomena.

In Britain, ghosts and hauntings are almost a national obsession but though connected in terms of the supernatural nature of the phenomenon; ghosts, are quite a different matter to professional mediums; spiritualism, channelling, or other more commercial forms of what would once have been called necromancy; often resorted to by the grieving living.

Spiritualism has been a cause of controversy, since Biblical times, when King Saul, (the predecessor to King David) visited the witch of Endor to get her to conjure up the spirit of the dead prophet, Samuel. In more recent times Sir Arthur Conan Doyle, the creator of Sherlock Holmes, (and as previously mentioned, advocate of the Cottingley fairies,) was a well known proponent of spiritualism; whereas the famous magician and escape artist, Harry Houdini, was an ardent opponent of 'spiritism' and believed it to be mainly conjuring tricks or hoaxes.

Whatever the truth of the claims and counter claims of mediums and their sceptics, it seemed to us that, in spite of its current popularity, too many question marks hung over the whole area of belief in spirits of the dead and their presence in our world. Like religious faith, it was a subjective product of human consciousness, the nature of which is still as much of a mystery as the nature of existence itself. Whatever was claimed about the after life, it was in the end a matter of personal belief.

We were in no doubt that there was a real phenomenon behind many of the authentic accounts of spirit manifestations but what exactly it was seemed very much open to interpretation; depending on what people believed. And as already postulated by others it is as equally feasible to view genuine mediums as unknowingly being empathic telepaths who draw their information from the emotionally needy minds who come seeking solace, as it is to see them as channels for departed souls. But either way there is, of course, the responsibility to help the grieving.

However, the whole idea of a 'supernatural' world, as opposed to, a natural world, is open to question. Before the advent of scientific rationalism the supernatural didn't exist as we conceive of it now. The boundaries between natural and supernatural were less distinct in ancient civilisations than they are today.

Within the popular world view of Medieval Europe, for instance; there existed many levels of overlapping reality. In Dark Age Europe, the reputed existence of faeries or demons was accepted as much as the existence of lions or bears. Strange events and otherworldly beings were an acceptable part of life in a cosmos that was seen to a large extent as multi-layered and essentially mysterious. In this view of reality you were either fortunate or unfortunate enough to encounter denizens from these other realms. In one sense they saw the whole of reality as supernatural. The world as it was then conceived of contained within it both the familiar and the extraordinary.

Our current dualistic view of the natural as opposed to the supernatural tends to prompt us to slot phenomena into one or other domain. But in effect both the 'natural' and 'supernatural' labels are merely subjective terms to describe aspects of existence. Useful, yes indeed; but perhaps whilst being aware of their function as descriptive labels, we should also be aware of their limitations.

If, for example, we were able to travel back in time and plonk a working television set in front of an intelligent family who lived during the Middle Ages, they would rightly consider the sounds and images produced by it to be a magical phenomenon.

This is simply because in the world as it was then, there were simply no reference points by which they could even begin to imagine how such a thing could be created or made to function. They would have no knowledge of the history of invention and discovery! (of which we are all subconsciously aware; even if we don't always understand it) Behind the technology of DVD recorders and TV remotes, which all children today seem to have an inherent knowledge of; is a history of invention: including: Alessandro Volta (1745-1827) creating the first electric cell; Michael Faraday's experiments, Samuel Morse's telegraphy, Edison's phonograph; Tesla's alternating current; and John Logie Baird's experiments, which collectively led to the cathode ray tube, and digital TV!

Our intelligent family of the Middle Ages would have been totally ignorant of all the basic knowledge they would need in order to comprehend television in any terms other than magical or supernatural. Not because they are stupid, but because they are bound by the limitations of their knowledge and by the prevailing view of reality at the time. In the world as it was then the technology to transmit images and sounds, miles through the air and manifest them on a screen, was not even conceivable let alone possible!

Today, in spite of its current popularity, the whole area of ghosts and spirits of the dead is still very much open to question – not that such phenomena; (like the working TV dropped in front of our Middle Ages family) doesn't exist – but if it does, what does it mean? Are our beliefs about what happens after death any more valid than how our family in the Middle Ages would probably view television?

Even so, we did consider the possibility that the orbs and luminosities we have encountered at Brackenbeck, were evidence of some kind of haunting or ghost phenomena, but everything we knew of our home environment and the phenomena itself made this seem highly unlikely. From the first moment of moving in, we have both felt at peace in our home. There is no emotional or psychic disturbance here apart from what individuals may bring with them.

Neither has the house has ever been 'haunted' in any traditional sense of the word; except by cats, who, as we all know have a reputation for seeing things not visible to us humans. Cats are often cited as being able to see, or detect, ghosts and spirit activity. Ours can certainly detect if there is chicken in the fridge but whether or not this has anything to do with the spirit of a departed chicken is open to question!

In one sense it would have been very convenient (and popular) to explain it all in terms of spooks but the fact was, this phenomena wasn't exclusive to us, like moths, bees and ants, it is everywhere!

Throughout history, people in most cultures have been inclined to believe in another reality beyond or parallel to our own, and in general this is seen as the supernatural world. We have peopled it with all kinds of entities and events we cannot explain; until it is littered with a multiplicity of spiritual, astral and etheric levels, crammed with everything inconceivable and inexplicable in our own reality. But what at the moment may seem supernatural to us may be nothing of the kind. Our perception of reality, like our Middle Ages family, may just be limited by our ignorance.

Still, a lot of strange phenomena happen in this world, and not all of it as simply explained as the sceptics would have us believe. The

Wright Brothers would never have flown if they had listened to the sceptics! Personally I'm more inclined to believe in a spiritual world than a supernatural one. The spiritual is woven into every facet of existence; it can be seen in a sunset, heard in the cry of an eagle or felt on the lips of a lover just as easily as in a holy place or meditation. Implicit in the symbolism of the orb, the sphere, the circle of life, is the continuance of existence. Inherent in winged forms is the symbol of transformation and transcendence. In terms of the human psyche both these symbols give hope of the transformation and continuance of consciousness beyond death.

When people we love die we often feel disconnected; and it is natural to feel the need for some kind of connectivity; to seek for some assurance of continuance beyond the material world. If you were to ask me if I believe in the continuance of consciousness beyond this reality; I would have to say emphatically, yes! But if you asked me if the dead speak through mediums, or walk in the night as ghosts, I would not be able to affirm that. Consciousness itself is after all, a great mystery. All I know is that sometimes there is something transcendent that shines through the individual human spirit.

Recently we heard a man tell of the time he went to a funeral of an elderly couple, who had died within days of each other. In the church two butterflies appeared fluttering over the coffins. Then later at the graveside, the same two butterflies fluttered above the grave until the bodies were laid to rest. After that they flew away into the sky. Everyone present commented on the unlikely appearance of two butterflies in November. The man saw it as meaningful. It was certainly synchronistic and symbolic. Caterpillars crawl. Butterflies fly. But inside every caterpillar is a butterfly waiting to get out. Metamorphosis! Perhaps inside every human being is a transcendent spirit?

Perhaps it depends on which nature we feed; the caterpillar or the butterfly; as to where we go next? As we photographed the shining winged forms flittering in the night, we wondered where all this was taking us. Continuing to research the phenomena we tried to keep a balance of wonder and reason. We now began work on the book though at times this seemed an ill-fated occupation. Because what we didn't have at the time was a clear explanation for most of what was happening, or any idea where the book was going in terms of conclusions.

The phenomena without doubt had a spiritual dimension but all things considered it didn't seem that the supernatural world of ghosts and spirits was going to help us much in understanding what was going on.

We had to look in other directions.

Critical Angles:

Question: Does the fact that the majority of orbs and luminosities appear in places and circumstances that have no direct association with the dead suggest that they probably are not, in that context, exclusively spirit phenomena?

Answer: Yes.

Question: If mediums were able to convey information from those they believed to be dead, but were in actuality still alive, does this suggest that the information is derived from a source other than the world of departed spirits?

Answer: Yes.

CHAPTER 15

LIGHT RODS AND STAR SIGNS

"Twinkle, twinkle little star, how I wonder what you are."

POPULAR NURSERY RHYME

"It is not known who first stated that the points of light we see in the sky, the points of light we call stars, are really objects like our own Sun, but situated far away in space at distances immense compared to those in everyday life."

SIR FRED HOYLE

The phenomenon that had begun simply with orbs, now included interactive luminosities and faerie-like forms, which added another wonderful, if puzzling element. But where, we wondered, was all this going?

By now our preoccupation with the phenomena had even begun to impinge on our work time – it's amazing that we got anything done at all. But apart from wondering where it was all going, we were mainly wondering what these light forms were. We had looked at natural explanations, plasma theory, even the supernatural; none of which, to us, seemed to offer any conclusive answers.

The faerie-like images almost seemed too incredible to be true. But there they were, as plain as whiskers on a cat! Fortunately the cats' behaviour was at least consistent – and they were still leaving only mice and shrews on the doormat, not hobgoblin legs or bits of sprite!

It was all very puzzling, but there wasn't anything dark or frightening about our phenomena; and sometimes we could not help but see the humorous side of it; especially in some of the photographs. There was an intelligence there that certainly seemed to have a sense of fun. The only thing I could compare it with was dolphins. That may sound odd, but we will come back to this thought later. At the time, we were looking around for any clues that may make some kind of sense out of what was happening.

One evening as we were walking by the stream, the cats, who'd come along for their own reasons, seemed to be interested in something not visible to us, on the bank.

It could have been a vole or other small creature, but we both felt thought there was something else around. Katie hadn't got her camera, but I had mine and took a couple of shots.

The result was a beautiful globe of light surrounded by smaller luminosities. (Photo. 45.)

Although it wasn't a winged-form, it was very faerie-like. however not long after this, we were  catapulted out of the misty realms of our preoccupations with faeries into the Science Fiction world of other dimensions!

One evening, while I was busy, Katie had gone out with her camera to see if she could get anything. It was a warm night and she always enjoyed being outdoors, whether or not there was anything unusual about. Here is how Katie describes what happened on the evening of Wednesday 14 July 2004:

"Once outside I was eager to make contact with our friends, as I now thought of them. I was in a happy frame of mind, feeling a kind of childish excitement.

Previously we had captured quite a few nice big orbs over the stream and I was soon crouched in a slightly elevated position by a birch tree, about 10-12 feet away from the laurel hedge, which overlooked the little wooden plank bridge. As I looked through the viewfinder, it revealed a white vertical strip of light, which took me completely by surprise. This was something new. Flash! I took the first shot. Remaining where I was I waited the three-second delay while the digital camera recharged. Flash! I took the next shot. The light was definitely moving along horizontally in front of the laurel hedge. This was amazing! Flash! I fired again, not expecting it to still be there, but it was! I took five shots in all before the light column vanished. I could hardly wait to go back inside and show John what I'd photographed!"

As soon as she got in, she excitedly wrenched me away from what I was working on.

We uploaded the images and looked in amazement at the sequence of photographs. (Photo. 46. a, b, c, d.)

They revealed a moving strip or rod of transparent light that was

brighter and thinner in places. Katie described it as hovering in the air, moving backwards and forwards horizontally. On closer inspection the 'light rod', appeared to contain as though in a tube, small globes or orbs at the ends. We used the 'un-sharp mask' tool, in Adobe Photoshop, to enhance the images. We could now see that the vertical column of light must have been over six feet high; as the laurel hedge is over five feet. The next day, using a couple of garden canes, we did a rough visual comparison of the height of the light column. (Photo. 46.X. shows the enhancement & Photo. 47. shows the height.)

This seemed to confirm that this 'light rod' was well over six feet from top to bottom.

But what was it? It obviously wasn't an orb or a faerie-like, winged form, nor was it similar to anything else we'd seen before. And the fact that Katie had taken five consecutive shots of a moving light form was both remarkable and totally at odds with the plasma explanation. We now had yet another mysterious angle added to our already puzzling phenomena.

One of our friends, who had a lifetime interest in UFOs, was equally intrigued when we showed him the images. Could this be some kind of portal? Had we experienced any missing time? We didn't think so. In fact we weren't sure what to think of this strange new phenomenon! Its appearance certainly made me think of Science Fiction tales of dimensional doorways and films like 'Stargate.' But of course, fiction isn't fact. Even though some Science Fiction yarns have foreshadowed later technologies and developments. The only thing we knew was that this 'light rod' didn't conform to any of what we knew of the phenomena so far. We now had a completely different mystery, but we also had a couple of ideas.

Perhaps, like the winged forms, it was another form of luminosity?

In view of our past experience of these things, it seemed to us there was a reasonable basis for this assumption. But in terms of intuition, the gut feeling that we both got from the faerie-like forms and now the sudden appearance of this, 'light rod', was that they were connected and actually alive in some way. Though, of course we had no actual proof of this.

All our conjectures about the consciousness of the phenomena; were, up to that point, based on our personal intuitive interpretation of circumstantial evidence.

Though we didn't realise it at the time the sudden appearance of the light rod heralded a new and dramatic turn of events, when, a few days later, the same thing manifested again.

This time Katie photographed the same or very similar 'light rod' zooming in from the field beyond the garden. It flew at about a 60-degree angle around the laurel bush. But this time it didn't hang around. (Photo. 48. a, b, c.)

Some people have said this one looks like a mini flying saucer, but I'm more inclined to think it's more a case of UFOs being in the eye of the beholder on this occasion. Although star gates and dimensional doorways had been previously mentioned and discussed, we didn't seriously consider them as a possibility.

However, after the coming of the 'light-rods' it was obvious that the faerie-like forms had stopped appearing, though we were still getting the usual orb-like luminosities.

A couple of other odd things happened around this time which may be worth mentioning here. One morning I woke up early and as I couldn't get back to sleep, decided to leave Katie sleeping while I got up and got on with some work. About 7.50am I went back into the bedroom to check if she was awake and would like a drink. Katie woke up with a start and seemed disorientated for a few moments.

Then, before I had chance to go and put the kettle on, she began to recount a dream she'd had. In the dream she'd been laying on the bed, unable to move a muscle; and she was staring up at the ceiling. Floating in the air above her were two large, dense black disks, like eyes, which merged into one large dark eye as it drew nearer to fill her field of vision. At first she felt a sense of panic, but then as the blackness surrounded her, a growing sense of peace and wonder quickly overrode her fear.

As the darkness dissolved she found herself looking upwards into a vivid blue sky in which hung a shining golden oval craft. She felt a sudden feeling of exhilaration, as though moving upwards...and

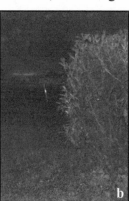

then… I entered the bedroom! The moment I sat down on the bed, Katie was able to move again, but the golden craft was gone! This dream seemed very real and made a lasting impression on her, especially the sense of being caught up into something wonderful.

We both already knew something of UFOs and alien abduction phenomenon and no doubt some people would indeed interpret Katie's dream in those terms. But we ourselves keep an open mind on this.

Through that summer we had a constant stream of friends and relatives staying.

We were now working from home and were very busy. Consequently, I was often getting behind with uploading some of the images off my camera memory cards.

The book was going reasonably well but it was far from finished. It was now the first week of November and after we had got back from an evening out, we were sitting on the veranda watching the night sky. It was absolutely clear and a brilliant night for star gazing. In the night sky opposite us we could see the constellations of Gemini, Cancer, Monoceros, Canis Minor, Orion and Canis Major, where Sirius, the Dog Star, was blazing brightly. As we watched the stars, out of nowhere came an even brighter light. This strange object hung in the sky above the treetops for a few minutes and then moved slowly off, out of Canis Major, to finally disappear in the direction of the Eridanus constellation. It was about the same magnitude as Venus and obviously wasn't a star or an aeroplane, or a satellite. I'm familiar with most things in the night sky and have had a long time interest in astronomy. As far as we were concerned it was most definitely a UFO, which is not to say it was extraterrestrial, just unidentified.

The very next morning, Katie was now anxious to see the backlog of shots that I'd still not uploaded, some of which dated back to September. As we looked through them, one in particular caught our attention. On this one the colours, sizes and the close formation of the orbs seemed decidedly odd. (See Photo. 49. a & b.)

The orbs on this one (49a,) somehow seemed less random than the rest, more pattern-like. Strangely Familiar. Something nagged at the back of my mind. What was it that was so oddly familiar about it? Not sure what I was looking for I began to flick through our backlog of images. Then Katie spotted it, another odd looking cluster of orbs. Why hadn't we noticed it before? Still, we now had two, but two what? (See photo 49b.)

Katie said, 'It's almost like we should join up the dots!'

A rather strange idea suddenly hit me, but I said nothing to Katie. Quickly reducing the two images to fit onto an A4 sheet, I printed them out. And going with my hunch I now made a tracing of the two orb groups I'd just printed. (See Figure H) Katie wondered what on earth I was doing. Then she caught on! We compared the tracings with the constellations on our star maps on the wall, but the scale was all

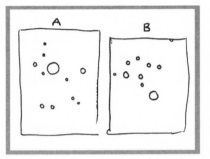

Fig. H

wrong – they didn't seem to fit anything. Pulling out our astronomy books, we began searching for similarities. It didn't take long before we found a match!.

We both stared in silent incredulity. The tracing of one of the orbs configurations almost fitted a diagram of Canis Major! Except there was a star missing.

But when we checked the photo, it was there! I'd merely missed off a faint orb when doing the tracing. The cluster of orbs now matched 11 out the 21 stars in the constellation Canis Major. And when we checked the date, this photograph was one of the ones we'd taken in September – but now it amazingly and coincidentally related directly

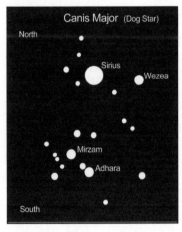

Fig. I

to our star gazing of the previous night when we'd seen the UFO passing by the Dog Star in Canis Major!

And even though I'd had reduced the image haphazardly merely to fit two photos on an A4 sheet, this image perfectly fitted over the star diagram in the book. The match to photo 49a was so close, it made the skin prickle. (Figure. I. Diagram of Canis Major)

Jung's concept of synchronicity and the astronomical odds against meaningful coincidences happening by pure chance seemed particularly relevant here.

Again the luminosities had demonstrated an incredible synchronicity and from our point of view, at that time, it looked very much like we were dealing with a phenomena that evidenced purpose.

But what exactly were we dealing with – aliens? Indeed at this point, we did discuss this possibility, particularly in the light of the Sirius connection, although as yet we have not found a star match for photo 49b. You are welcome to try your luck.

Over the years I've often followed space exploration missions and tried to keep an eye on local solar events such as planetary alignments, the appearance of comets and sun spot activity. And unlike some more orthodox stargazers, I do have a long term interest in UFO phenomenon. It's still a very controversial area, but the evidence for a percentage of UFOs being of non-terrestrial origin is definitely worth more than just passing consideration.

All that we've described above; moving light-rods, strange lights in the sky, orb configurations which turn out to match star constellations; would instantly spell out: ALIENS, in large letters, in the minds of some people. And it is a possibility that we have considered – and then rejected, in this instance. Although we must point out here that we do not reject the idea of Aliens; or of an Alien presence in our solar system. But that is a different matter to what we are dealing with here. The more we reflected on the whole spectrum of our phenomena, the more we felt that it was probably no more conclusive to write this off to the mysterious activities of elusive ETs than it was to slot it into the misty world of ghosts and spirits.

Luminosities, in certain specific circumstances, undoubtedly could appear like spirit or alien activity. But they couldn't be both – not unless ghosts drive flying saucers. Just as with the mediums who had contacted dead people who subsequently turned out to be living, there was something else going on. Taken in totality there was something other at work in the phenomena of luminosities than aliens or spirits. Something, which perhaps could pick things out of our minds and reflect them back to us? In the midst of all this we had to keep reminding ourselves that this was more than merely the photographic phenomena. That was just the finger pointing at the moon, not the luminosity itself. If we wanted to understand the phenomena we had to travel beyond the images. Travel to where the finger was pointing. It was the meaning behind the phenomena that we were after. So far we had seen orbs, interactive luminosities, faeries, moving light-rods and star configurations all nicely depicted for us, at a time when it was just dark enough for us to see the light. And that of course was one of the three main connecting links, across the whole phenomena: Light! That and synchronicity. And running through it all from the very beginning was something so small and familiar, that it is often taken for granted by those people who experience it: Small Transient Light Phenomena.

Spirits, ghosts, aliens: these are not everyday phenomena; but for thousands of people, all over the world Small Transient Light Phenomena is!

Could there be something else living along side us? Why do the aliens, reported by abductees, or contacted by channellers always seem so interested in our welfare and the state of our world? Could it be because they are us – products of the human collective unconscious? Or because they are connected to us, sharing this world with us? All things considered, our gut feeling was that whatever was manifesting itself as luminosities, faeries and star signs, was not from some vague abode of the dead or some distant galaxy; it was right here with us.

We had just begun to think along these lines when suddenly the lights literally went out! There were no more photographs of orbs, nor luminosities of any kind. To all intents and purposes the whole phenomena had gone away.

Critical Angles:

Question: Does the appearance of a vertical column of light that moves horizontally suggest the possibility of a three dimensional phenomena?

Answer: Yes.

Question: Is the fact that a tracing of an orbs configuration; almost perfectly matching the stars in the constellation of Canis Major, where the previous night we'd seen a UFO in the same constellation; suggestive of the possibility of a conscious purpose at work?

Answer: Yes.

CHAPTER 16

LIGHT-FORMS

What is the way to the abode of Light? And where does Darkness reside?

Job, 38.19

We went out, taking photographs as usual, for nearly two weeks, but during this time we photographed neither orbs nor any other kind of phenomena. In the context of our previous experiences this was a decidedly odd state of affairs and we were not only feeling perplexed, but abandoned by the familiar luminosities.

Had they now gone for good? Deserted us? Why had the phenomena stopped? We didn't know! But then, one day, as suddenly as it went, it came back. And this time not only luminosities appeared. There was something else; something quite different; something incredible. This is how it happened.

At three-thirty in the afternoon the sky was awash with the effects of a burning autumn sunset, sending beams of golden light streaming through our long windows to land across Katie's desk. As it got darker she couldn't resist the urge to go out again and see if the luminosities had decided to reappear.

As I was in the middle of some design work, I said for her to go ahead and see what she could get. Pointless probably, I thought, even though Katie was quite optimistic. So, leaving me working, Katie took her camera and headed out into the dusk to try her luck again. She had done the same for the past few nights but with no results. This is how she described the events that evening:

"Once out, I stepped lightly through the grounds, along with the cats, happy to be outside in fresh air and to be light and free once again. This evening I felt a sense of expectation. For some reason I just knew they were back! From the middle of the drive, I took my first shot between the trees, high into sky and sure enough was rewarded with a big sparkling light! 'Hello, again!' it seemed to say! The next couple of shots seemed to bring it closer. There was no doubt that the luminosities were here again. Moving through the garden, I took shots in all my favourite places: by the stream, on the bridges, in the woods and by the wild cherry tree. And in all those places I was now seeing lots of white sparkles of light. There was no doubt about it, the luminosities were back! Overjoyed, I knew we were making contact again. It felt like a game of 'Catch me if you can'. In the Fairy Dell, I stopped and looked around. The cats were sidling up beside my legs; they too seemed happy and frisky. I too felt a childish sense of happiness at just being out in the night, shooting into the dark again.

Speaking out loud I said, 'OK, no more hide and seek, now. I'm going to take my last shots right here, so come on!' The next minute the viewfinder was filled with a white light that shocked my visual senses as the flash hit whatever it was, making me jerk the camera away. Had they responded to my words? I felt washed with light. It was all around me. I could feel it! The hairs on my head and legs prickled, with static. I called out; ' Yes! Keep on coming!' but the barely visible wisps of light moved away. It was hide and seek all over again. I followed using up my last few shots. Then they were gone back into the night or to wherever luminosities came from. I returned inside to show John what I'd seen."

When Katie came in I could instantly see that something extraordinary had happened and when she told me about the definite presence she'd experienced, I grabbed my own camera and went out to try some shots, but I got nothing at all. Whatever it was had gone. Coming in, we now looked at the incredible shots that Katie had taken.

What Katie had seen, she described as being like a fluctuating electro-static white light; and as her images showed she had photographed something much more exciting than our old familiar orbs.

(Photo. 50.) It was a totally new form – a Light-form!

Looking at her shots, I was amazed and excited by the dramatic misty images. They seemed to be almost alive! Curling, twisting shapes, lit up in the night by the photon bombardment from Katie's camera flash.

The next night we both went out with our cameras. Katie was

convinced that if we called them verbally or mentally then these new light-forms would respond – and amazingly they did! One of my favourite shots is the one showing Katie enveloped by a curling, misty, light-form, and right there with her are the luminosities as well.

(Photo. 51.)

In case anyone is tempted to write these images off simply as mist, there was definitely no mist that night, nor at any of the other times we photographed this new manifestation. And also we had been out on numerous occasion before (and since) in the same conditions and got nothing at all.

Some may think that we may have created these forms in some way. We haven't.

What you see in these photographs is as it appeared. Sceptics are welcome to try and reproduce the effect. But as soon as we had got over our initial excitement we did begin to look at any possible natural causes ourselves. We quickly eliminated the possibility of the obvious: ground mist, rain or smoke. Could it have been our own breath? We did some tests to deliberately take shots of human breath in the night air. We either got nothing or what we did get, though obviously misty was shapeless and formless, certainly nothing at all like the dynamic vaporous forms we were photographing. Even so, we now made a point of holding our breath, whenever we took a shot. Not that this made any difference, many of our subsequent shots continued to reveal an

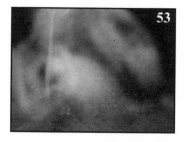

abundance of white misty vapours, dancing, twirling, leaping; some immense in size and often filling the photo frame. Occasionally they had a hint of colour. (Photo. 52.)

Most of the swirling shapes made no sense in human terms, but sometimes we and the friends who saw them, couldn't help but make out familiar images within the misty shapes. One, for example, is reminiscent of a horse's head. (Photo. 53)

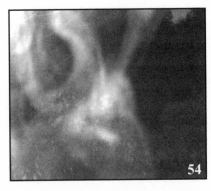

Another is like a winged creature or insect. (Photo. 54.)

But of course they are probably none of these things. It is more likely to be our own human eye seeking to see the familiar in the unfamiliar. Unless of course, these images were meant to trigger particular visual connections?

The opinions of our friends varied, some classing them as vapours, some as apparitions. But in effect no one knew what they were. At times the shapes, or 'light-forms', as we had now come to call them, seemed to be twisting and moving in some flowing kind of dance. The images themselves had an almost organic quality. But the really interesting and exciting thing for us was that they seemed to be responding and interacting with us as individuals. It felt at times as though we'd connected with another consciousness!

Now more than ever the experience felt more like a union; a sharing of the joy of being. Katie felt it very much like a time of communion with an energy that often filled her with a sense of wonder. It was almost magical. However, as excited and enthralled as she was by this phenomena, Katie, one day, explained that she was now also concerned. The cause of her concern came from a book she was reading at the time on the Dead Sea Scrolls. The Biblical references had reminded her of her Church of England school days; her confirmation and earlier beliefs. The book spoke of; 'following the path of light' and of 'coming out of the darkness into light'; dark being the familiar metaphor for those things associated with evil and light traditionally meaning righteousness, goodness, truth and all things of God.

Intellectually she knew that fundamentalist interpretations of scripture were flawed. Their doctrines often being slanted towards keeping the believers from thinking too much, keeping the flock together in fear of straying. Nevertheless Katie had to ask herself the question: were we being led astray?

Was it possible that, the strange things we were experiencing could be, as they say in Star Wars, of the dark side?

Let's try and put this question in some kind of perspective:

Anyone who encounters the extraordinary and paranormal must at some point question the nature of the phenomenon they are dealing with. Is it good or is it evil? How do we define what is one or the other? Is some one else's definitions of any more value than our own? As we look at this question, we mustn't forget that paranormal phenomenon isn't just the province of odd people with weird beliefs; or of New Age conferences or cults. It underpins the very fabric of every religious institution in the world. The everyday beliefs of billions are founded upon the common acceptance of certain paranormal events. Strange phenomena has plagued, added to, or inspired all the major religions throughout history. In fact some beliefs have come into existence precisely because of an individual's encounter with unusual phenomena. Roman Catholicism, for instance, absolutely abounds with tales of miraculous events, apparitions and visions: some of which border on the outright grisly and frightening and seem to be more like some of the occult practices, which the church itself condemns. In earlier times the church would have relegated luminosities to the pit along with elves and demons. But if we are ever in danger of believing that any single religion, then or now, is the sole divinely appointed arbiter of what is good or evil, it is well to remember what history has to teach us about religious ignorance and stupidity. At one time even sausages were considered by the Roman Church to be the work of the devil!

And anyone who cooked up any ideas on anything contrary to official dogma was dealt with very severely, especially if those ideas, like those of Galileo and other fledgling scientists, impinged on the official view of reality. Fear has always been the bed-fellow of fundamentalism; and it is fear which impels men to evil deeds.

Galileo, who had his eye on orbs of an astronomical nature, was brought before the Inquisition in Rome 1633 and forced, under threat of torture, to recant his 'false' view that the Earth moved around the sun! Before Galileo, only 33 years earlier, the visionary writer Giordano Bruno had already been burned at the stake for daring to teach the new Copernican view that Earth was not the centre of the universe. We look back at this now and think; what an evil thing the Inquisition was, but such was the consequence of ignorance and religious dogma.

If the history of world religion teaches us anything, it is the sad truth that those who claim to have received the truth of God from the hand of angels have often behaved like demons! This is particularly relevant today, because when the phrase 'fundamentalist fanatics' is used, most people generally think of Islamic fundamentalists. But it's worth remembering that it's not so very long ago, historically, that much of Western Europe lived in fear of the religious fanatics who made up the Roman Catholic Inquisition. Fundamentalism of any description is always bad news for human freedom and those seeking after truth.

When it comes to the question of truth – as to what is good or what is bad; duplicity has long been a characteristic of most major religions. Even recently in the US presidential elections, the same evangelicals who were coming out against abortion, because it was against the sanctity of life, were also advocating capital punishment and military action in Iraq! And such is the strange and illogical power of belief that many who unquestioningly accept transubstantiation: that in Holy Communion, bread and wine can literally turn into the body and blood of a man; cannot accept that: UFOs, aliens, clairvoyance or the ability to see auras, are anything other than the work of the devil, or the results of a delusional mind.

It would seem that in some circumstances both science and belief can blur our perceptions of reality.

Personal paranormal experience is usually looked upon with suspicion by both science and religion. The individual lives in a world of systems, religious, political and economic. And sometimes, when personal experience runs contrary to the commonly accepted views of the majority – the majority get nervous!

It is well for us all to remember the importance of individual experience. The basis of Judaism, Christianity and Islam could, in one sense, be said to be the result of individual paranormal experiences similar to today's accounts of precognition and alien abduction. And interestingly, all three religions of the 'Book,' hold in common the belief that the truth was handed down to the prophets by celestial, non-human intermediaries.

There has been something, some other level of reality, interacting with ours throughout human history. The results of some of this activity has been later diluted, repackaged and turned into religions. And yet, even in spite of systematised beliefs, there is something in the human spirit that is unquenchable. However, the unquestioning adherence to dogma, whether religious or political, blunts individual creative thought and keeps humanity down and crawling. Fortunately inside us all is the underlying force of that higher Being of Light, that butterfly of the spirit which is seeking to fly!

When we see winged forms, anywhere, humans may also see a metaphor, a sign of hope, of aspiration to a higher level. So too when we looked at the winged images we had photographed we saw something which spoke to us of the ascendancy of the spirit. In the orbs and luminous spheres we see the symbols of oneness. And in the swirling dynamic manifestations of the light-forms we see joy and transformation. These images, we believe, at one level speak directly to the spiritual aspect of humanity.

Even so, most Christian fundamentalists we have spoken with on this subject see this type of phenomena, like aliens and spiritualism, as the work of the devil.

Unfortunately dogmatic adherence to some beliefs, do close the mind and dull the individual spirit; which in any real terms is all any of us truly own. If we give this part of us away to be chained up or enslaved to another will, we own nothing.

Anyone who is a slave to anything is no longer free.

And it is interesting to note that some of the world's greatest thinkers, such as Apollonius of Perga, who laid the foundations for modern geometry; Hippocrates, the greatest physician of antiquity, who is regarded as the father of medicine; and Democritus, the philosopher, who developed the atomic theory of the universe and Pythagoras, who invented the famous theorem named after him; all lived in ancient Greece, in times when there was no over all authoritarian religious perspective, to stultify the freedom of thought!

In terms of man's spiritual endeavours, throughout history, in spite of times of prevailing rigid dogma, there has been a whole spectrum of paranormal phenomena, including signs and symbols, luminosities and light beings, which have contributed to our spiritual quest as human beings. Perhaps helping us each to discover and release the beings of light inside us all.

In discovering the truth for ourselves, each of us must first listen to the voices of our own personal experience, reason and intuition, before we listen to the views of any belief system. For all of us ordinary mortals, it's always worth remembering that whatever grandiose claims any one group may make on 'the Truth', when it comes right down to the bottom line, all you are dealing with are individuals who are as prone to human failings as the rest of us. Perhaps when John Lennon said 'follow no leaders' he wasn't too far off the mark? One of the great teachers of the last millennium, Krishnamurti, actually discouraged people from becoming "followers". Perhaps he knew the dangers of trying to organise spirituality.

It could be said that practically everything in life has a spiritual component. This is especially true for any personal paranormal phenomenon, because often exposure to the unknown results in life-changing experiences and the expansion of personal conscious-ness; which always has spiritual consequences. Our own luminosities and light-forms were no exception. Katie's doubts as to their nature were dispelled by the light of thought and reason, and personal experience. All our experiences of the light-forms had been positive ones and the presence of the luminosities in our lives had set us on a new spiritual quest for meaning beyond the commonly accepted views of reality.

In the three years that we had been exploring our luminosities, we had been perplexed, intrigued, excited, but never afraid. And as we now looked at the recent images of these dramatic new light-forms, we felt a tingle of expectancy; a lifting of the spirit. What we were looking at was something totally new.

It was almost as if they wanted us to see and feel that they were alive! Showing us, perhaps that they were much more than a two dimensional image.

These light-forms were so  unlike anything we've ever seen before. Even more than the winged-forms, they seemed to be offering us a glimpse into another realm of reality. We were now sure that something 'Other' was visiting the garden and woodlands of Brackenbeck; and it was making us strongly aware of its presence as a conscious entity. What exactly it was we didn't yet know. But whatever it was, we both instinctively felt it was good and had as much right to be here as we did. They may come with the night, but what we were seeing and photographing were forms made of light!

As we studied the images, we wondered if what we were seeing were what other people would call angels or spirit beings? (Photo.55.)

Could this perhaps be what had given rise to some visions of angels?

Today there is a world wide interest and belief in angels. What are angels?

In the New Testament, the word angel comes from the Greek term angelos and literally means messenger. In the Old Testament the word translated as angel is malak and also means messenger. In both instances the word angel, describes only the function of the being; it is simply a messenger of God. The concept of angels is derived from the ancient civilisations of Mesopotamia and from New Testament Christianity. But today angels are viewed as transcending any one particular religion; they are seen as beings of light or pure spirit. The Bible speaks of guardian angels and as well as being messengers of hope this is still seen very much as their function today. There are numerous interesting books written about angels and their meanings and it is not within our remit here to delve into the whole spectrum of beliefs surrounding them, except as it may relate to our own light-form phenomena. Could our light-forms be manifestations of angelic beings?

It is quite possible that they could! In terms of the original meaning of the words malak and angelos, an angel is simply a messenger, usually celestial, so in that context our luminosities and light-forms could be said to be angels; for they had been continually giving us messages on various levels, as to the fact of their existence. If anyone wishes to think of luminosities and light-forms in that sense, it is perfectly all right with us and will not be out of keeping with the spirit of the phenomena! For in all their transitions, from orbs, luminosities, to winged-forms and light-forms they had always felt good and positive. There had always been an unearthly celestial aspect to the phenomena from the beginning.

Some times the dynamic shapes of the twisting, curling light-forms seemed almost like dancers acting out a ballet. (Photo. 56.) Telling a story to their audience. But even though we had

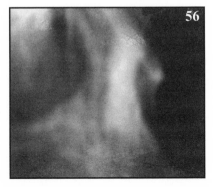

56

front seats at this light show, we still didn't yet understand the meaning behind the actions. Interestingly we were now both thinking, in terms of 'them', as though they really were an intelligent non-human life-form. Light-forms! In my own experience, there was only one thing with which I could compare this feeling of being in the presence of an intelligent non-human consciousness.

I'd only once ever interacted with a dolphin, and then only for a short time, but it was enough to convince me that it had both intelligence and a sense of humour.

Dr Horace Dobbs, who founded International Dolphin Watch, often speaks of this sense of intelligent playfulness in dolphins. And it was this pervading sense of playfulness; which time and again we had felt and seen in the behaviour of our luminosities and light-forms. It was something which did the spirit good; that lifted one up beyond the cares of this world, where we clump around on our boots of concrete and steel. We felt lightened in hearts by this phenomenon of light.

Something that may or may not be relevant, but which seemed so to us, was that looking back on our photographs we realised that many of our key shots had been taken in the vicinity of the little plank bridge. This was where Katie had seen the moving light-rods and where we'd photographed the orbs pattern which matched the constellation of Canis Major. Was this coincidence? But once one starts with synchronicity, meanings pop up everywhere.

Still it was interesting that one of the light-forms (photo 50) just happened to look like a bridge, and a bridge is a link between one place and another. It seemed an interesting analogy – but maybe that is all it was. We certainly weren't short on possible creative connections, even if we were short on actual answers and as yet still didn't understand it all. But in spite of our lack of real definitive knowledge, somehow the shadows of doubt over what we didn't know, seemed to be dissolving.

Though we didn't realise it; somewhere in the dark the sun was rising and we were about to see a new world.

Critical Angles:

Question: Does the appearance of new moving, dynamic, shapes of light that now appear consistently in place of the faerie-like forms suggest a transition or evolution of the phenomena?

Answer: Yes

Question: Does this new aspect to the phenomena evidence an interactive consciousness at work?

Answer: Yes.

CHAPTER 17

THE LIGHT BEING

"Light. One light. Light that is one, though the lamps be many."

(THE INCREDIBLE STRING BAND)

Since the coming of the light-forms, life at Brackenbeck had, outwardly, continued much as before; inwardly it was a different matter. Most of the time, although we were supposed to be working, our thoughts were on our strange phenomena. What was it? What did it mean? Mentally, we were continually mulling it over. We now had a few clues and one or two exciting possibilities.

Please bear in mind that we have no special knowledge and don't claim to be: messengers of the gods, ascended masters, walk-ins, alien hybrids, or any other kind of spiritual super-beings you may sometimes find running courses at New Age conventions or Mind, Body, Spirit festivals. We are just ordinary people who have encountered something extraordinary - all we have to go on are our personal experiences, our reason, our imagination and our need to discover the truth of it all.

But how does anyone discover the truth about the unknown?

The fact is, as Sherlock Holmes would no doubt agree, the unknown is never quite as unknown as it may first appear; we always know something about it; even if it is only that it is, unknown. So what about our case in particular? Well, there were certain things that we definitely knew about our phenomena and certain things that we now suspected about it. First, here is what we knew:

1. It began as orbs.
2. It is sometimes visible as Small Transient Light Phenomena.
3. It is photographable. Therefore it must exist in the visual spectrum.
4. As orbs and spherical luminosities it shows the physical behaviour and properties of plasma concentrations.
5. It has the ability to change form.
6. Throughout the whole range of the phenomena, from orbs to light forms, there has been an element of specific interaction in its behaviour.
8. Synchronicity has been a constant factor pertinent to the whole phenomena.

Our inklings, based on what we knew can be summarised as follows:

a. Small Transient Light Phenomena is either the visual form of the phenomena or a by-product of it.
b. If that is so, then it is pervasive everywhere – not just at Brackenbeck.
c. It is conscious and responds to human thoughts and/or emotions.
d. For some reason it is interacting with us as individuals.
e. All its activities and expressions suggest it has purpose.

This was all very well, but we had all but abandoned: aliens, ghosts and the supernatural in general as explanations. So what were we left with – faeries? This seemed highly unlikely as the actual truth behind the phenomena; and anyway it had now moved on from faerie-like forms to the more complex swirling organic shapes of the almost angelic light-forms.

All things considered, it seemed quite likely that the faerie-like forms, like the orbs, were a phase; perhaps another form of whatever it was that had decided to visit us. Throughout all the aspects of our phenomena we had sensed a kind of playful intelligence that, as I've already mentioned, reminded me in particular of another non-human intelligence: dolphins. And as I said in the previous chapter, I had only ever interacted with a dolphin once but , that was enough to convince me that it had both intelligence and a sense of humour.

One of the worlds leading experts on dolphins, Dr Horace Dobbs, of International Dolphin Watch, often speaks of this sense of intelligence and playfulness in dolphins; something which we had consistently felt in the behaviour of our phenomena.

Could looking at dolphins offer us any clues as to what we were dealing with?

Dolphins are the intellectuals of the sea and are, according to most experts, at least as intelligent as humans. Some would even say more intelligent. They are not only capable of problem-solving they are also capable of initiating behaviour and have a well known sense of fun. They are probably the only other mammalian intelligence on this planet comparable to humans, though some would not agree with this because dolphins lack arms and legs, the ability to make fire and have no technology. Though it would seem that the view of; 'if it's not the same as us, it can't be intelligent', is in itself a rather unintelligent viewpoint.

Because something is 'Other' than us, does not mean that it is less than us, just different. Dr Dobbs has often talked about what he terms 'ambassador dolphins'. These are usually lone dolphins who seem to deliberately come into bays and inlets to seek interaction with humans, often over prolonged lengths of time, such as the one in Dingle Bay in Ireland. And it is very interesting to speculate that whilst men are out at sea studying dolphins, these ambassador dolphins are perhaps deliberately coming into our shores to study us.

Many people who work with dolphins affirm that they give of a positive energy; some would even say a healing energy. The Japanese call it Chi energy, and as we know, this is the energy symbolised by the Tai Chi or the Yin Yang, as the expression of the dynamic interaction of opposites, of harmony and balance, set within the circle of Oneness.

Our thinking had taken us from orbs to light-forms to dolphins and back to the symbol of Oneness: the circle - the orb!

Could it be, I wondered, that we were perhaps in a similar position to those humans who have met ambassador dolphins – were we being visited by friendly but curious emissaries from a non-human intelligence? Astounding as this may sound, was it possible that this is what lay behind the tales of faeries, ghost lights, aliens and other strange light phenomena that seems to deliberately interact with humans at times?

That oft used quote from Shakespeare, about there being more things in heaven and earth than are covered by any one person's view of life, had always seemed to me to be worth bearing in mind when thinking about the incredible and the unusual; and it became even more pertinent in what happened next.

THE LIGHT BEING

One evening, as we returned from one of our frequent forays around the grounds looking for luminosities and light forms, something even more exciting occurred.

It had been a clear, dry night, but we had not got anything. As Katie looked for her key, I pressed the 'off button' to switch off my Pentax digital camera. Except that I didn't. Instead, by mistake, I pressed the, 'shoot button'. Unexpectedly the flash went off. Katie had opened the front door and was going inside. I glanced down at the screen and what I saw made me call Katie back. We both stared in disbelief at the image on the camera; then at each other. Even on the small screen it was obvious there was something odd on the veranda. 'Quick – take another one!' she said.

I did so, but it was my last shot and Katie's camera was out of battery. We hurried inside, eager to see if it really was what it looked like on the camera screen.

When we looked at the images on the computer there was no doubt what I had taken. There on the veranda was what looked like a

figure of luminous vapour!

Surrounded by a thin cloud of mistiness, it was hovering between the cane chair and the woodpile, its posture reminiscent of someone moving forwards. (Photo.57.)

Almost two and a half minutes must have passed between this first shot, taken by accident, and the second, taken deliberately. (Photo. 58.)

But on the latter shot there was no

mist, no figure, nothing. The veranda was empty. The night, as you can see, was clear and dry, with no mist at all. Though not as dramatic as the dynamic light-forms, this image was particularly more exciting simply because it looked so human like.

Perhaps we humans are just more easily impressed if we see non-human entities that look something like us, instead of something completely alien.

Certainly something that seems partly human and partly something else does seem to fascinate us. Perhaps if something looks slightly human we are more likely to accept it as both non-human and intelligent.

Humanoid light beings are recurring images in both Sci-Fi films and UFO phenomena. And we now had one practically strolling along our veranda. This was an amazing turn of events. When much later we showed this image to people; some of whom, we knew had themselves, had out of body experiences or alien encounters, they all, almost without exception, recognised it as a 'light being'.

This incredible image, whilst welcomed by those who had seen similar beings themselves, did have its disturbing aspects. Theorising about alien or higher intelligences is one thing, when you are dealing with a phenomenon with no visual human attributes, but when it suddenly turns into a form that looks humanoid, that is something else entirely. Even as a means of communication, it says very clearly that it shares aspects in common with humans. Not least the

59

ability for parody.

Its appearance seemed to con-firm to us that perhaps we were on the right track with the notion of a non-human intelligence making contact, in much the same way as the ambassador dolphins were said to do. Is that where all this had been leading, preparing us for the appearance of humanoid looking light beings? Certainly over the next few weeks we did get a few more images of what appear to be the same or similar kind of light being. (Photo. 59.)

We have others, which at this time, we cannot include here. But that is not the end of the matter. Suffice it to say that though it would have been nice to think that the luminosities had all along been leading us to a reality where human-like beings of light existed; somehow it still didn't feel quite right. Not completely the whole story.

It felt too neat! And though we were now photographing these 'light beings', we were also still getting orbs, odd luminosities, faeries and light-forms as well! Whatever it was, obviously either hadn't finished yet, or we were too stupid to see what it was telling us. But we were in little doubt that this light being, even as just an image, spoke directly to the spirit within us. We felt lightened by its presence. It recalled to us that just as every caterpillar has a butterfly inside, so we each have a spiritual nature within us, a nature which impels towards transformation. If we humans are spiritual children, then perhaps the adults are not too far away?

THE IMAGE

Late one afternoon, a couple of months later, I happened to take a shot of Katie in the Faerie Dell. Uploading the images, later, it we noticed something unusual in the top right hand section of one of them. (Photo. 60.)

This wasn't an orb, nor a light-form, not even a light being, this time we were looking at something that looked, for all the world, like the top half of a statue! When we enlarged and enhanced it, it looked even more statue-like. (Photo. 60A. Enlargement)

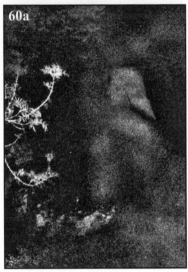

This image looks definitely artificial. Unlike the light being, there is nothing alive looking about this image whatsoever. It looks like a representation. But in terms of the history of strange phenomena, this image isn't at all unique. There have been many oddly anthropomorphic images both seen and photographed: Like the giant image of Jesus photographed in the sky during a bombing mission in the Korean War. (Fig. J.)

Or the photograph of a shining Madonna-like figure seen in a tree in Metz, France, or the image of the Virgin Mary in a piece of burnt

Fig. J

toast, sold recently on Ebay.

One of the most unusual of these oddities was the appearance of the image of the face of Dean Liddell of Oxford, in a patch of damp on the cathedral wall, years after his death. None of these odd images are ghosts or apparitions; just random elements which happen to coincidentally form human-like images that are recognisable or have meaning. It may well be that our image is also in this category and that it is no more than a trick of random light and shade which just happens to look like a statue at the moment of photographing.

But taking all that into consideration, if we then look at this image in the context of all that had happened so far, was it possible it could have some meaning?

As we thought through all that had occurred, all that we had photographed, since the orbs first appeared, we began to get an inkling of a possibility. If this image was not just a random collection of pixels, if it was from the same source as the other phenomena, in that context, what was it likely to mean?

Well, for one thing, the statue-like image obviously turned the mind towards art and images, simply because it looked so artificial. We began to think it through.

All that we had experienced so far suggested a non-human and non-material consciousness at work. So, taking for granted that we were actually dealing with non-human intelligences, what if this statue-like image really was what it appeared to be: an image of a representation. What could that mean? Could it be saying, for instance, that the light-being was an image of a being, like a statue is an image of a person, not the actual being itself?

In the almost surreal world of light-forms, it seemed to make a strange kind of sense. Art and images, whether paintings or photographs; are first and foremost a means of communication. Had the intelligence behind the light forms been using natural forces such as plasma, visible light, atmospheric conditions and so on to manifest itself?

Was it possible, that if a consciousness was involved; that it could have taken things that were familiar to us and played them back as visual presentations, or generated synchronistic events and interactive responses?

We pursued this line of thought a little further. Other things seemed to slot into place. For instance, we were both interested in astronomy – so we got star constellations! We'd both, in the past, produced designs incorporating faerie images, and Katie was particularly interested in children's fairy stories – so we got something faerie-like! Katie had once had a meaningful predictive dream – so we got a manifestation recalling a dream image specific to Katie!

STL, the Small Transient Lights Phenomena had been such an

influencing part of Katie's own personal spiritual quest that it could not be coincidental that both orbs and luminosities just happened to be connected to it; or that we had both synchronistically witnessed the same light effects when we each first came to live at Brackenbeck, where practically all our other phenomena have occurred. There did seem to be a lot of connections here specific to us as individuals.

Put in that context, it all seemed to make a strange kind of sense.

Katie's passion since leaving school had been painting and since moving into Brackenbeck she had begun to revive her career as a contemporary artist; was it coincidence that we have witnessed an array of visual phenomena that pointedly centred on the pivotal aspect of art – communication! After nearly four years of visual puzzles, was it possible that the statue-like image held the key?

If there really is a non-human consciousness that shares this world with us and that this intelligence exists as a non-physical energy, like Chi, could it be possible that it could connect with human consciousness at times and manifest itself in forms and events meaningful to individual humans, but which are not necessarily the true forms of this consciousness itself? Was it further possible that this consciousness was demonstrating that everything we've seen is a form of communication by a non-material, non-human intelligence that is as real as we are? If so, then by implication this intelligence knows far more about us than we do about it! Nor would this kind of consciousness be restricted to the material three-dimensional world we are bound by.

If what we have encountered and photographed here is the same phenomena that throughout history has given raise to the world wide reports of luminosities, ghost lights, faeries, even perhaps some alien abduction cases, then it would seem to be an intelligence, which has been connected to humanity for a very long time. In that context although able to manifest in our material reality, they more than likely also exist at other levels, undetectable by us.

Perhaps they (and we feel it is a "they", rather than an "it") are, like humans who traverse the seas, able to move through the ocean of our existence, passing through or manifesting in our environment for their own purposes? If higher none material intelligences do exist, perhaps like the ambassador dolphins, some are, at times checking us out? Or perhaps some are on a mission, trying to help material life forms develop into higher spiritual beings? Perhaps they are not alien at all, perhaps they are what we may become?

These were interesting possibilities - if the level of reality of the light-forms is as different to ours as, say, our level of existence is different to the world of bacteria; then perhaps we should not be too surprised that much paranormal phenomena is totally inexplicable! Especially if what we consider paranormal is a by-product caused by the overlapping of realities. If, as reported throughout history, the light-forms are active here, do they affect human consciousness?

In the context of what we'd learned so far, it seemed likely that they did. Perhaps they are intimately connected to us and our level of existence in ways that are almost beyond our comprehension.

Many who look at our images of light beings will inevitably think of aliens like the entities in the film Cocoon, or they will think of ghosts and spirits. Not that we don't think either aliens or spirits exist, or will eventually be proved to exist. All we can say is that in our particular case neither aliens nor spirits felt right, nor seemed to fit the over all context as we saw it.

Our view is that:

1. All over the world the occurrence of orbs and luminosities is increasing.

2. Orbs and luminosities have been shown to be the photographable form of Small Transient Lights A phenomenon which seems to be ubiquitous.

3. In our own particular case, faerie-like forms, light-forms and light beings are all directly connected to orbs and luminosities; which are aspects of a phenomenon which can manifest in a variety of forms.

4. This phenomena is generated by, or is the expression of; a non-material intelligence.

   The question is: who are they?

Critical Angles:

Question: Does the appearance of a humanoid light being, necessarily mean that this form is anymore a true visual representation of itself than are orbs, faeries or light-forms ?

Answer: No.

Question: Can we show a probable connection between all the major aspects of our own phenomena, such as: visible transient lights; photographable light phenomena; personally meaningful synchronicity and specific response to individuals?

Answer: Yes.

Question: Does all that we know to date of the phenomena, historically, personally and world wide, imply that it is generated by a non-material intelligence?

Answer: Yes.

CHAPTER 18

THE QUESTION OF PHENOMENA

"I've learned to take everything on board, because you never know when it may become relevant to some other strange event"

COLIN ANDREWS, CROP CIRCLE RESEARCHER

Since the dawn of time they have been with us: spheres, orbs, strange luminosities and beings of light. Extraordinary light phenomenon has a long history all over the world.

Especially the orb-like luminosities; seen in visionary encounters, dreams and the human subconscious. Luminosities, light-forms and light beings have not only been critical elements in many individual paranormal experiences, they have been present at the foundations of some of the world's major religions and beliefs.

The Bible, the Koran and the Hindu Scriptures all contain references to visual symbols and phenomena which are very much akin to the luminosities, light-forms and light beings seen by ordinary people throughout history. If you take the trouble to look through the archives of most newspapers worldwide you will find that references to fireballs, spheres and strange luminosities crop up fairly regularly from about 1840 onwards. In 1905 the Sydney Herald had many reports of glowing spheres or fireballs. In 1938 the Daily Telegraph reported glowing spheres that were seen by many readers during an unusual display of the Aurora Borealis over England. Luminosities and light-forms of various types are also documented as being associated to spirit phenomena, hauntings; alien abductions; and they also appear in accounts of near death and out of body experiences.

Luminosities are not only extraordinary phenomena: welcomed by believers and dismissed by sceptics; they are also a very familiar phenomena to many humans throughout the ages. In fact, paradoxically, sometimes so familiar that their existence is almost taken for granted! We humans are great compartmentalises, we like to stick things in nicely labelled boxes, just so that we'll know where to find them next time. Orbs, luminosities, faeries, light-forms and light beings are generally filed away under various separate and diverse headings, depending on their context, such as: aliens, the supernatural, spirit manifestations, ball lightning, natural phenomena, religious visions etc. But if we disregard the context in each case and look at the properties and behaviour of the phenomena itself, we begin to see glaring similarities.

Luminosities/light-forms begin to take on quite a new meaning if we view them all as aspects of essentially the same phenomenon, which is perhaps the manifestation or expression of a non-human consciousness, sharing this world with us.

Could it just be possible that we are not the only, nor the most intelligent form of life on Earth? Is it possible that there is something that we have missed?

Wherever you are at the moment, look around; how many people are there?

It doesn't matter if you are in a café, at college, at work or in a supermarket, no matter how many people you see, they are the minority of life forms in proximity to you. The majority of life forms on this planet are generally unnoticed or invisible. Insects; bacteria;

germs - on the ordinary, everyday physical level, these creatures outnumber us millions to one. And it's no good saying: so what! Only humans really count because they've got bombs and digital TV! Wrong!

An atomic war could wipe out the whole human race, but the majority of insects would still survive. And in terms or our survival, if it wasn't for the trillions of invisible friendly bacteria we would all be dead. It's a mistake to think something is of no consequence simply because we don't know it's there most of the time. Some of the most dangerous organisms on this planet are microscopic – just think about the pandemics of the past that wiped out millions of people and how in our present everyone is panicking over Avian Bird Flu. In the everyday world that we all take for granted, we live in a reality that has many overlapping levels, full of myriad invisible life forms, most, if not all of which have a direct bearing on our existence both as a species and as individuals.

The truth is, human societies are so intensively human centred and so demanding of our time and attention, that the vast majority of us are only vaguely aware, if at all, of the wider reality of which we are only a part. Could it be possible that just like the ants in our garden, who are unaware of us as individual beings, let alone the vast, ecological, spiritual, political and economical world that we inhabit; that we too are totally unaware of other levels of reality? Levels that are perhaps as interconnected to ours, as ours is to the creatures who inhabit our garden? The various creatures of which, are, by-the-way, totally unaware that it is a garden at all!

Our eyesight can detect only a fraction of the electromagnetic spectrum; even at just the physical level there is much more we are naturally incapable of seeing than that which we can see. What about other levels of reality, beyond our detection at all? As we pass through any room in our homes, we are moving through an environment that contains millions of microbial life forms; none of whom are capable of registering our existence as individuals. Though of course, our presence, if it impinges on their level of existence, will disturb and stimulate them. We and the microbes share the same world, but at vastly different levels of reality. Is it possible that something 'Other' than us exists which at times moves through our world leaving a trail of inexplicable phenomena which are but the signs of its passing?

Is it possible that there is another level of reality inhabited by non-material beings, who are as different to us as we are to microbes?

Some people look at dolphins and think they are fish simply because they have flippers instead of hands. Other, more enlightened people, see them for what they are; intelligent sea-dwelling mammals. Others recognise something in them beyond the form. They recognise an intelligent consciousness – and try to understand it; try to communicate with it. That is what conscious beings do; try to communicate with others who are not them. That is what the SETI program (the Search for Extraterrestrial Intelligence) was all about: It was an expression of our need as a species to find and communicate with something that is not us.

Some would even say that this is why humans reach out for God, or the Great Spirit or to angels or aliens, or any other number of cosmic entities.

It is almost as if there is a need inside of us that is programmed to look for and seek to communicate with something that is not us. Higher life forms, maybe? Are we impelled to transcend our physical existence; is this the butterfly nature inside the caterpillar, seeking to fly? Looking for its natural habitat? Communication with another level of reality runs throughout all beliefs everywhere on the planet. It is almost as if, like radio transceivers, our brains, our minds; our consciousness even, has been designed to search for something beyond this reality.

Throughout history individuals, mystics, religions and adherents to all kinds of beliefs have been tuning in; through meditation, prayer, personal experience; scanning the frequencies; listening; trying to communicate with something Other, something that transcends our ordinary human reality. Why? Could it possibly be that we, like the ants in our gardens, are part of a wider reality, which includes a non-human consciousness to which we are drawn and possibly connected? Is it possible that to a non-material higher intelligence we could be as limited from their perspective as dolphins are from ours?

No matter how intelligent a dolphin may be, the fact is, in human terms, it lacks the physical capabilities for creativity and technology. It lacks the ten digits we have. Because of that it cannot exist outside of its environment; unlike us it cannot take a minimised version of its environment with it. We can dive into the alien environment of the seas and survive. But no sea-dwelling species can survive in our environment; not without our help. Do we need help? All religions say we do.

It may be totally inconceivable to some that a non-material higher intelligence exists, or that there may be other levels of reality. But the fact is, to a goldfish; the world beyond the goldfish bowl will also be as inconceivable. Yet it is there. Could it be that in spite of believing ourselves to be the most dominant species on the planet, we are like the dolphins, highly intelligent, but limited by our physical parameters?

Less flattering, are we also, at another level, like microbes, limited in terms of our perceptions and consciousness?

In trying to understand the light-forms we have had, of necessity, to look at the question of consciousness. There are certainly aspects of human consciousness not explicable in accepted psychological terms; these include precognition, telekinesis and telepathy. According to some psychologists, even synchronicity, in spite of Jung, is not considered to be real! Recently, at a conference, we listened to a speaker, in giving an illustration of a point, told the story of how he had once had access to his children refused on the grounds that he was a schizoid personality. When he questioned the female psychologist, as to why she had made this diagnosis, he was told that it was because he believed in Chi energy; which she did not consider real, consequently her assessment was that he was living in a delusional world!

In the kind of closed, egocentric mindset evidenced by this psychologist; Jesus, Buddha, the Dalai Lama and over half the population of the world, would all be wearing straight jackets! Chi energy is one of the most well authenticated and widely used forms of non-material energy. Its existence, under various names is recognised by many beliefs and it is fundamental to many martial arts and ancient practices such as geomancy and acupuncture.

However such unenlightened mindsets as the female psychologist was set rigidly into; are merely a result of the fear of anything different that is so prevalent in orthodoxy of all kinds. Acupuncture, which is more than 5,000 years old and based on the concept of Chi energy, has been widely and successfully used; recently patients have even had open heart surgery by use of acupuncture.

During the writing of this book; we noted that orthodox medicine is now reluctantly admitting that acupuncture may actually work. Amazing! That will be comforting news for all those who have practiced it successfully for the last 5,000 years!

The fact is practices like acupuncture are usually frowned upon because they are based on a totally different concept of reality than accepted in the West. And as we can see from the case of acupuncture, because something is not acceptable to us or cannot be scientifically proven, doesn't mean that it isn't real!

In terms of pursuing our speculations regarding the existence of another level of reality, from where we believed our light-forms and other paranormal phenomena may originate; it may be interesting to now look at Chi energy.

Chi energy, like the paranormal, is thought not to exist by most orthodox scientists and psychologists. But whether they like it or not, millions will testify to the very real existence of a non-material energy, which lies behind tried and tested practices such as: Acupuncture, Reflexology, Colour Therapy, Shiatsu, Kinesiology, Ayuravedic medicine and martial arts such as: Tai Chi, Aikido and Kung Fu.

CHI ENERGY

The idea of Chi is based on a whole different concept of reality than is understood by Western science; and is far older than any of our present notions of reality.

Essentially in the ancient Chinese view, the fundamental connecting energy of the universe is known as Chi. This energy flows through everything on this world and in the universe beyond. It connects everything. But it is not a physical energy, like magnetism, although it flows through and affects all energetic systems. In the human body Chi energy flows through it in lines of force called meridians and is most particularly concentrated in energy centres known as Chakras; of which there are seven, designated by the seven colours of the rainbow. Interestingly for us the small transient lights which Katie often sees, over or near to people; are predominantly pinks and purples, perhaps reflecting the violet shades of the Crown chakra, which is the highest spiritual centre of the body, and which is, coincidentally, known as a doorway for spiritual communication. This seems quite appropriate in the context of our theories on our phenomena. Others, who also see small transient lights, also report these colours in association to people. When viewed as prana, this energy has been said to often be visible as myriads of twinkling lights. Exactly the same phenomenon that Katie and many others have seen. Once again we have a possible Chi connection.

It is Chi that empowers the energy fields around the body, which are collectively known as auras; and which can be seen by some adepts. However none of this is acceptable to orthodox science as it cannot be tested or proved scientifically according to our current understanding. And yet still amazingly to some and, not surprisingly to others; Chi energy works!

What can be verified scientifically is that human bodies are bio-electro-chemical in composition and that all brain processes are essentially electromagnetic. Because of this human beings are affected by both direct and indirect exposure to external electromagnetic fields. Depending on the degree of exposure, these effects can be both physical and emotional, sometimes with dramatic results.

Those who accept the reality of Chi energy would also attest that the human body, when energised by Chi, is capable of amazing feats; producing both physical and mental effects; on other people and even on animals or objects.

Years ago, I attended a workshop on Chinese martial arts. This particular session was taken by a very old and wrinkly Chinese gentleman, who was a master of Tai Chi Chuan. During the course of the evening he asked the strongest man in the room to try and move him. This man was over six foot three and looked like Arnold Schwarzenegger's big brother. The little Chinese man was old and frail-looking and hardly five foot two. Any betting person would have naturally thought the odds were way in favour of the younger, bigger man. How wrong they would have been. All the little Chinese man did was stand with his arms by his side – but no matter how hard the strong man tried he just could not move the old man so much as an inch. None of us could! How could this be?

In purely physical terms this makes no sense whatever. It would seem totally unlikely that a big strong man in his mid thirties could not move a small frail man in his seventies. Something else was at work there, which was not explicable in terms of the commonly accepted everyday physics. Not bad for something that orthodox science tells us does not exist. What else may exist that we are told is impossible; another level of reality? A higher non-human consciousness; perhaps even light beings?

For those who may have no practical experience of Eastern concepts of Chi energy there is a simple experiment that anyone can try, to show that the ability to move objects is not always relative to brute physical strength. This is an interesting one to try with your friends. To do this you will need five people. The subject sits in a chair, while the other four attempt to lift him in the air by placing their index fingers under his arms and knees. This naturally proves impossible. The four people now place their hands on top of his head in a pile, the first one placing his right hand on the head, followed by the next person's left hand, followed by the third person's right hand and so on until all have both hands in a pile on the subject's head. They should then all concentrate very hard on imagining lifting the subject out of his seat for about 25 seconds, then at a given signal simultaneously remove their hands from the head, place their index fingers under the knees and arms and lift. This time the subject will effortlessly rise into the air. Impossible, Yes! But it works. Why?

Another indication that there is a universal consciousness woven throughout the material world is the effectiveness of psychometry. This is the practice of deriving information from inanimate objects about either the dead or living people who may have been associated to them. This is something anyone can do, with varying degrees of success, though naturally some are better at it than others. All you need to do to try it is have someone give you an object to hold that you know nothing about. It can be anything. To start with it is better that you don't see it, to prevent your logical mind from making wrong associations; so do it in the dark or blindfolded. With your friend present, hold the object for a few minutes but don't think about it all. Think about something else. Let your hands feel without thinking. Whatever odd thoughts or impressions you get popping into your head; say that out loud to your friend; even if it seems to make no sense. But it is important that your friend, who does know about the object, makes no comments one way or the other. At the end of about 20 to 30 minutes or so you may be surprised at how much you got right about something you knew nothing about.

Some so called paranormal abilities, such as psychometry and telekinesis are quite probably connected to, or part of, Chi energy, which in itself is probably connected to, or is the expression of non-material forces that exist at another level of reality. Research into all kinds of paranormal phenomena strongly indicate that at times we may interface with some form of energy not dependant upon the laws of physics as we currently understand them. Interestingly at those times and places, where positive thought, or psychic or spiritual activities are taking place; many people have reported seeing exactly the same kinds of small twinkling lights that Katie sees. This is a visual manifestation of prana or Chi energy and evidences a link between this energy and many types of extraordinary phenomena. Small and large light phenomena are often associated to visionary experiences, sometimes exotically so, as witnessed in Fatima, Portugal, in 1917.

In the context of our own phenomena this is a particularly interesting case because it embraces both luminosities and light-forms.

MIRACULOUS LUMINOSITIES

There have been previous accounts written on Fatima and for those interested in the whole story, we would recommend that you read those. For the purposes of this book we shall only look at those aspects that relate to our own phenomena.

Commonly believed by Roman Catholics to be a miraculous appearance of the Virgin Mary; the incident at Fatima centres around three village children who, on 13 May 1917, were out watching sheep, when they saw a bright flash. Walking towards the luminosity, they found themselves caught in a bright light, which almost blinded them. In the centre of the light they saw a being of light, which was later described as a small woman. The light being spoke to them and bid them to return every month to the same spot. Quite naturally this tale caused much interest amongst the superstitious locals.

On the second appearance of the apparition, there were fifty other people present as well as the three children, most of whom were also local Roman Catholics. This time the children appeared to be in the presence of someone invisible to the spectators. At the end of the encounter, witnesses all heard a sound like an explosion and saw a misty luminosity rise from the vicinity of a tree. On the third appearance, on 13 July, there was a crowd of 4,500 people watching as the three children listened to someone invisible and most of the crowd again saw some kind of misty, cloud-like luminosity near to, or raising up from, the tree. On the fourth appearance on 13 August, although 18,000 people were there; the children were not. They had been kidnapped and jailed by a local official who wanted to put an end to what he termed "nonsense".

Even though the children were not present the light phenomena still played to the crowd: there was a bright flash of light and a clap of thunder in the air. The misty luminosity was again seen by the tree, and rising into the sky. Witnesses saw coloured lights like rainbows near the ground and luminosities in the sky around the sun.

On 19 August there was a fifth appearance; the children, now released, were out tending their sheep as usual. The landscape was flooded with all the colours of the rainbow, and although this time there was no waiting crowd, the phenomenon was visible to other people in the vicinity and attracted witnesses. The children saw a bright flash as a glowing luminosity came and settled in a tree near to them. In the centre of the luminosity was again a being of light, which was later described as a lady dressed in white and gold. After 10 minutes of communing with the children; this lady of light and her luminosity floated off in an Easterly direction.

On 13 September there was now a crowd of 30,000 to witness the appearance of a globe of light that floated down the valley and came to rest on the tree by the children. Out of the empty sky appeared many glistening globules which, as they fell upon on the crowd, got smaller the nearer they came. When people reached out their hands to touch them the globe-like phenomenon just disappeared.

Again the children saw the lady of light inside the luminosity. Each time the apparition had appeared and spoken with the children, it had made predictions to return and given promises of a miracle on 13 October. And so when the apparition manifested the last time, there was a crowd of 70,000 people to witness its appearance. Again there was a flash of light, again the luminosity descended into the tree; again the children spoke with someone invisible to the crowd. Again the phenomena included the appearance of luminosities and extraordinary atmospheric light phenomena.

The Miracle at Fatima, over its various appearances, was witnessed by thousands and testified to by hundreds of believers and sceptics alike. According to the children's testimony the lady of light, who was actually seen only by them, was described as a "little woman". Each time the luminosity appeared, in which this lady of light arrived, it consistently settled in the top branches of the same small tree. And according to the children, the feet of the lady of light rested on the top branches. Both the lady and the cloud-like luminosity were described as being small. How small?

Putting the observations together and allowing for distortion by distance or eyesight, it would seem that the luminosity was a sphere about four or five feet in diameter. Inside that was the lady of light. In that context she probably would have been much smaller than a normal human. Putting aside the Roman Catholic associations to the Virgin Mary; in other circumstances this lady of light could have easily been described as a faerie apparition or a white lady ghost. And stripping away all the contextual religious connotations, what are we left with? Something with essentially the same attributes, as the familiar light phenomenon that has been variously described as; faeries, ghost lights, ball lightning, spirits, UFOs and aliens, by many throughout history.

Is it possible that events like Fatima, though translated by humans to fit current beliefs at the time; are attempts at overt mass communication by intelligences from another level of reality? Most of these paranormal communicators have seemed distinctly concerned about us as spiritual individuals, our possible future as a species, and our planet's ecological future. Which raises the question as to whether or not they have a vested interest in us? Perhaps the phrase: "we are not alone" has a meaning much closer to home. Perhaps we don't need to wait for the arrival of visitors from a distant star to meet with an alien intelligence. Perhaps it is already here!

Critical Angles:

Question: Does the existence of paranormal phenomena suggest that there is another level of reality impinging on our own?

Answer: Yes.

CHAPTER 19

THE QUESTION OF CONSCIOUSNESS

"We are all flowers in the Great Spirit's garden. We share a common root and the root is Mother Earth."

GRANDFATHER DAVID MONONGYE, HOPI

We have looked at our luminosities and light forms and tried to explain them, first in terms of natural causes such as lens flare or dust; and found most, if not all, of those explanations inadequate in the circumstances. We have viewed our own particular luminosities in the context of other light phenomena, such as plasma concentrations, ghost lights and the supernatural and found certain similarities but no definite answers. We have looked at our luminosities and light phenomena in general, in the wider context of synchronicity and symbolism and found that luminosities are actively connected to both those aspects of consciousness. Looking at diverse accounts of other paranormal light phenomena relative to our own experience has led us to speculate that most of the diverse light phenomena which includes orbs, luminosities, light-forms and light beings: whether faeries, aliens or spirits; are all manifestations generated in our world by the activities of a non-human intelligence. And that this intelligence exists at a level of reality that impinges on, or perhaps coexists with, our own.

This led us to question: What is this intelligence? Why is it here? What is its purpose in manifesting itself to us and to many others throughout history so consistently? Before attempting to try and answer questions about a non-human consciousness, we must first delve deeper into the question of human consciousness itself as this is the means by which we perceive both the normal and paranormal.

Apart from the fundamental question that philosophers have struggled with for eons; "what is consciousness?", we must, of necessity, here content ourselves with the fact that it exists, and move on to look at how it may influence our perceptions of both the normal and paranormal.

SOME THOUGHTS ON CONSCIOUSNESS

In his work on the conscious mind and the individuated self, Jung originated two concepts that have been shown to have a bearing on paranormal phenomena: they are: the collective unconscious, and synchronicity. We have already touched upon synchronicity in Chapter 13 and seen that it is a fundamental connecting principal. Synchronicity is at work through all levels of life and has been of particular relevance in our own experience and encounters with luminosities and light-forms. The existence of synchronicity implies that we do not live in a universe of random chaotic events and that consciousness is somehow bound up with matter, not separate from it but woven through it. In a nutshell: chance doesn't exist and consciousness has purpose! Furthermore the existence of synchronicity implies and qualifies the existence of the collective unconscious, and vice versa. What is the collective unconscious?

Jung created the term "collective unconscious" to define a layer of psychic activity below the level of personal individuated consciousness. In the level of the collective unconscious are stored all the past common experiences, wisdom and fears of the whole human race. Sometimes these experiences surface into the conscious mind as dreams, symbols or intuitive insights. The collective unconscious is where archetypes come from; these are the pre-existent primordial underlying forms that keep recurring in the thoughts and expressions of human consciousness. The circle and what it symbolises could be said to be an archetype. The concepts of both synchronicity and the collective unconscious have a direct bearing on the meaning and existence of: dreams, hypnotism, past lives, precognition, telepathy and other psychic abilities.

To visualise an individual in terms of synchronicity and the collective unconscious, we could, as an example; take Leonardo's Vitruvius man as representative of a single person in the circle of his life from birth to death; which for us is always experienced as the present.

If we draw four larger circles; (one pair to represent the collective unconscious past and future, and the other to represent past and future synchronicity) so that we have two circles touching the original circle horizontally, and two vertically; the man in the circle of his present is now like the pupil of a double eye.

If we could then transfer this image to a computer; turn it into a 3 dimensional object; then multiply that, say, one million times, so that

Fig. K

all the larger spheres overlapped each other, we'd have a small graphic representation of how synchronicity and the collective unconscious interconnects an individual life to other lives, past and the future. (Fig. K) In the synchronistic world the individual exists in a web of interconnected spheres of events, which connects him to every other individual his life touches. Implicit in the reality of synchronicity at work in individual lives, is the notion of some kind of connectivity of consciousness below the level of everyday personal awareness. In psychology this is better known as the collective unconscious.

Of course, in the everyday world of physical existence; graphs and theories about the synchronistic connectivity of consciousness are not facts. So, is there any demonstrable physical phenomenon that shows not only the connectivity of consciousness, but actual physical results of that connectivity? Yes, there is!

PRIMARY PERCEPTION

On 2 February 1966, Cleve Backster, one of the world's leading experts on polygraphs and the originator of the Backster Zone Comparison Test; the standard test used by lie detection examiners all over the world; decided to link a plant up to a polygraph. The results were astounding. Subsequent experiments showed that plants, like humans, responded to emotions: to love, to threats, and to fear.

Backster discovered that within a few hours plants would become attuned to the humans in their vicinity and pick up on their emotional content. As the plants, which were hooked up to the polygraph, responded to human emotions, the reactions of the plants were displayed on the polygraph printout. Backster and his team found that plants, which had formed no attachment to humans when put in a strange environment and connected to the polygraph, began to look around with their limited perception, for some emotional activity to latch on to. As plants didn't have most of the first five senses, Backster coined the term: "Primary Perception" to describe what was happening. Which was that on a primary level; plants seemed to be empathising with, and registering human emotions and intentions. Further more, he later discovered that this Primary Perception went right down to the bacterial level; with one pot of yoghurt, registering when another pot was being fed. Cleve Backster's research showed that both individual plants and bacteria would go into a state of shock to protect themselves, particularly if members of their species in the vicinity were being eaten, or threatened with death. But when the danger was past the plants or bacteria would register normal again.

Backster believed that this cessation of electrical energy at a cellular level was similar to the state of shock people enter into in cases of extreme trauma. In furthering his work on Primary Perception, Cleve Backster later began to work with animal and human tissue. He discovered that sperm taken from human donors, when put in a test tube and hooked up to electrodes, would register response to the activities of the donor; even though the donor was several rooms away. Taking cell samples from human bodies he then found that these cells would react to the emotional responses in a donor's body, even when the person in question was 20 miles away!

In different area of study, another researcher, Rupert Sheldrake, simultaneously filmed both dogs at home and their owners at work. His experiments showed that even when the owners came home from work at a different time each day; at the exact moment they left work; back home, the dog headed for the door!

Both Cleve Backster and Rupert Sheldrake's work strongly imply, if not clearly evidence, a connection of consciousness throughout the plant, animal and human world. This was intriguing.

But was there a possible planet-wide connective matrix within which a connected consciousness could exist and express itself? Again, yes, there was!

THE GAIA HYPOTHESIS.

This may be well known to many of you.

The "Gaia Theory" first came to the world's attention in the book: Gaia: A New Look at Life on Earth by British chemist, James Lovelock. In ancient Greek mythology, Gaia was the Earth goddess; the mother of all living things. In his first book, Lovelock put forward the argument that the earth has the characteristics of a living organism.

In support of this, Lovelock cites many examples of the activity of planet-wide processes which ensure the stability and conditions necessary for Life. These processes are called homeostatic processes. An example of this is that the concentration of oxygen in the atmosphere is always at 21 %; the planet's surface temperature, always at between 15 °C and 35 °C; exactly right for living organisms; added to which, the ammonia content of the lower atmosphere and the ozone layer of the upper atmosphere are naturally balanced at levels conducive for the survival of life.

The homeostatic processes functioning all over the planet are so many, so varied, and so finely tuned that, in Gaia theory, only the concept of a planetary organism can explain them. In this view of the whole world as an integrated organism, humanity is not the focal point; merely a part of a larger system, very much like the ants in your garden are part of the environment of the garden. Left to itself the Earth, as a self-sustaining planetary organism with interconnected living systems will regulate and perpetuate the conditions favourable to organic life. However, in the Gaia Hypothesis, it is possible for things to go wrong, for systems to break down, due to outside interference such as asteroid impacts; or to the long term nefarious activities generated by humans. If the earth is a self-sustaining organism, it may also be self-adjusting; and in that case both air pollution and destruction of the equatorial rain forest may well provoke a corrective response from the Earth's bio-systems.

Lovelock was the first person to show that Chlorofluorocarbons, (CFCs) were accumulating in Earth's atmosphere. This resulted in worldwide movements to try and ban the pollutants which would deplete the Ozone layer and create dangerous greenhouse gases.

For years James Lovelock has been warning the powers that be of the dangers we all face if we don't stop polluting the planet.

In the first part of the 21st century world leaders, especially in the West, are now probably wishing they had all paid more attention to Lovelock years ago. Politicians and industrialists are only just waking up to the real possibility that we live on a planetary organism, which pays no more attention to presidents and world leaders than we do to individual ants in our garden.

In recent months, climate change, global dimming, the tragedy of the Indonesian Tsunami, as well as mega-hurricanes and earthquakes have galvanised the attention of the world's media. These days, films like The Day After Tomorrow are reinforcing in the human psyche that perhaps we are all not as invulnerable as we once thought we were.

If the Gaia hypothesis is correct, these events could be symptomatic of Earth's corrective systems coming on line! However, Lovelock's Gaian theory is all about planetary biological systems; it is about the Earth sphere as a biological machine, and how the surface of our planet operates like a huge organism. As far as we understand it, Lovelock in no way implies a planetary consciousness by his Gaia hypothesis. But, of course, as far as we are concerned, the whole concept of the Earth as a living organism; seems to offer the ideal habitat for a planetary consciousness. In one sense the human body itself, could easily be viewed as a biological machine, which it undoubtedly is; but, as we all know, it is also a vehicle for consciousness.

A PLANETARY CONSCIOUSNESS?

There was a lot of food for thought here, especially linking the notion of Primary Perception and the probability of a connection of consciousness across species, to the idea of the Earth as a living organism. Perhaps even a conscious organism? This turned our minds back to Jung's concept of the collective unconscious and to the occurrences of synchronicity we had experienced with our own phenomena. Was it possible that some kind of planet wide consciousness was behind it all?

When the faeries and light-forms appeared we had begun to look at the possibility of a wider, non-human, consciousness; how that may be connected to what was happening with us in particular and to the manifestation of paranormal phenomena in general. Each new experience and encounter we had with our light-forms had drawn us further along the road of questioning our commonly held perceptions. It seemed that we now had two possible strands which strongly indicated a connectivity of consciousness in both normal and paranormal phenomena: They were:

1. The reality of synchronicity at work in everyday human lives and the probability of a collective human unconscious.

2. Both our own experience, and the experience of others in general, of paranormal phenomena is

suggestive of another, non-human, consciousness interacting with ours.

If we think of these elements, for a moment, in terms of children's Lego building blocks; we can now slot the human collective unconscious piece and non-human interactive consciousness together; and then plonk them both onto the new shiny piece of Primary Perception; if we then slot all three on to a block which represents Earth as an interconnected self sustaining planetary organism, we have the foundations for an integrated worldwide matrix of consciousness that could generate both normal and paranormal phenomena.

This idea is not new (except for the Lego). Long ago ancient spiritual teachers spoke of the connection of all things and of the Oneness of mind, body and spirit.

We believe that it is highly possible, that as well as being a self-sustaining biological machine; the planet itself could have a conscious matrix, to which all living things are connected. But if it did, how would we know this?

What could be the effects of this consciousness as far as we humans are concerned?

Taking into account all that we know of the Earth as a living organism, it seems likely that if it does have consciousness, it most likely operates in the background, just like the human collective unconscious; and expresses the out workings of that consciousness through its living systems. A consciousness-driven biological organism would strive for balance and harmony: and would be capable of being self-adjusting, very much as attributed to Earth as Gaia. In fact in Gaian theory the Earth operates very much like a living body.

CHI ENERGY AND EARTH CONSCIOUSNESS

There are similarities in this idea of a planetary consciousness to ancient beliefs about the Earth-body. In the Eastern perspective, which gave birth to Tai Chi, Yoga and Acupuncture; the human body has an interconnected system of meridians, or energy channels through which flows the vital life force, or Chi.

In Chinese Geomancy, from which Feng Shui is derived, the Earth is seen as the counterpart to the human body; with an interconnected web, or lines, of life force running through, and over it. Many people will be familiar with these energy lines as Ley Lines. In Chinese geomancy they are called "dragon paths"! They connect the Chi energy that flows through the Earth in a similar way to which Chi energy flows through the human body. The Tai Chi symbol, the Yin and Yang; Light and Dark; is the symbol of opposing forces balanced in harmony forming a circle, which is itself the symbol of perfection and eternity; the symbol of the Earth, the symbol of flow and connectedness; Oneness.

In the Earth-body model, the planet is viewed holistically, with each part of every level reflecting the fundamental nature of the whole. For example; just as the Earth is made up of various physical layers, which radiate energy fields, so too the bodies of all Earth creatures are multilayered and radiate individual energy fields.

Auras and energy signatures are detectable in all living things.

Chi energy flows through all the bio-systems of earth; the flow of this energy forming a dynamic interconnecting web, similar to the meridians in the human body. In that context we would expect there to be planetary nodal points where this energy is concentrated, just as in the human Chakras.

At a purely physical level we would expect the energetic

by-products of a conscious organism to be detectable; in much the same way that we can tell that the human mind is there and functioning, by monitoring electrochemical and electromagnetic activity in the brain. And indeed, there are definite points around the world where geomagnetic energy is exceptionally intense and where strange phenomenon repeatedly occurs, and affects human consciousness.

In ancient Chinese Geomancy, this energy system, the Earth's meridians, are well known and respected. In this understanding dragon paths and ley lines are part of the Earth's network of Chi. In this context geomagnetic phenomena, is an indication of the positive or negative functioning of the Earth's energetic grid. Just as in the body, Chi energy is vital to life and harmony, at every level of existence, throughout the entire planet.

PLANETARY MANDALAS

Ever since we photographed our first orbs we had been discovering circular connections. When we looked at human consciousness; we discovered mandalas as symbols and expressions of the human need for integration of the self; for Oneness. Then looking at the Earth in terms of a planetary organism, we could see that the same symbolism which is repeated in the circular evidence of crop circles; may well have meaning. If Gaia, as a living system, has consciousness; crop circles could be the equivalent of mandalas, drawn by the Earth itself. Perhaps they are expressions of a planetary mind rather than oblique messages from aliens? These symbols appear not only in crops but in the tops of tropical rain forests, in deserts and in ice fields; and in countries all over the world. Maybe we would understand these mysterious and spontaneous visual forms better if we thought of them like mandalas; as the out-working of a living consciousness?

MAGNETIC PULSE

It is only in the last century that scientists began to realise how fundamentally humans are connected to the planet on which we live.

The Earth has its own distinctive magnetic pulse, and it is now known that anyone blocked from the Earth's pulse by electro-magnetic interference can become very ill. Because of this, NASA uses magnetic pulse generators to replicate the Earth pulse on all space craft that carry astronauts. Energetically, as well as biologically, we are connected to Mother Earth.

CONNECTING ENERGIES

What about consciously? It is a well known fact that paranormal phenomena occurs more often and more intensively in the vicinity of ley Lines and those places where, according to the ancient Chinese beliefs, lines of Chi energy cross. Could it be that in places where the Chi energy of the Earth is more concentrated that our own individual consciousness is more affected by the planetary consciousness; resulting in strange or visionary experiences?

Is it possible that the Small Transient Light Phenomena, seen by thousands all over the world; is the visible manifestation of a ubiquitous consciousness?

Could Chi energy itself be a by-product of such consciousness, or perhaps even the energising spirit that powers it? Either way, Chi energy has been effectively channelled by humans and shown to be directly connected to consciousness itself. If the Earth is a super-organism, through which Chi energy flows; then it seems likely that a planetary consciousness exists and that we are affected by it.

There are many invisible forces that have been shown to directly affect our perceptions of reality; not only according to controversial theories, but according to mainstream scientific research. The human brain, for example, is highly sensitive to electromagnetism, particularly parts of the temporal lobe. Here is located the hippocampus; the lateral ventricles; which are the parts of the brain related to dreaming, memory and language. Research suggests that the hippocampus acts like a transducer of electromagnetic energy. Stimulation of these areas can produce out of body sensations, floating feelings, hallucinations and even mystical visions. Concentrated magnetic fields can directly affect our consciousness and perceptions of reality.

In fact, whenever we walk through the landscape of the Earth we move through invisible areas of natural radiation, gravity anomalies and geomagnetic fields, all of which have an affect on us; usually minimal but sometimes very acutely.

And this is just at the bio-geophysical level. What about psychically or spiritually?

If we align the ancient view of the Earth as expressed in Chinese geomancy, where Chi energy permeates and connects the whole natural world to the notion of a human body, suffused with a web of interconnecting meridians of that same Chi spirit energy; in that context, we have an energetic and spiritual connection with the planet we live on.

A relatively recent discovery which seems to validate ancient views on a connective energy flowing through all living things is that of Kirlian photography; by which pictures are produced, showing the colourful energetic emanations of living organisms. Invented in 1939 by electrician and amateur photographer, Semyon Davidovich Kirlian and his wife Valentina, the process which bears their name has demonstrated that human bio-energy fields exist and shown a connection between the photographed energy discharges and the Chi energy points and meridians on the human body.

In spite of orthodox scepticism, Kirlian photography has also proved itself as a diagnostic technique for all type of illness. The electrobioluminescence effects shown up by this process have been affirmed by some researchers to be evidence for the existence of a bio-plasmic body which is what ancient teachings had been describing for thousands of years as the invisible fields of astral, mental and etheric energy, exhibited in the auras of all living things and directly empowered by Chi or prana which connects the Earth and all its creatures.

If the animating spirit of the Earth is aware and interactive, could it manifest itself through paranormal phenomena in general, and more particularly in our own case, through luminosities and light-forms?

Critical Angles:

Question: If both the Gaia Hypothesis and the theory of Primary Perception are correct does this indicate the possibility of a Planetary Consciousness?

Answer: Yes.

Question: If a Planetary Consciousness exists and if both synchronicity and the Collective Unconscious also exist, does this suggest a connectivity of consciousness, throughout all levels of all life on Earth?

Answer: Yes.

CHAPTER 20

THE CIRCLE OF LIFE

"Whether superorganism, organismic community, or just plain orb, the planet is ingenious at converting refuse to refreshment."

LAWRENCE E. JOSPEH. *GAIA The Growth of an Idea*

"It is one of man's illusions that the oceans and land masses of the world are eternal and that he himself is the end product of billions of years of evolution."

JACQUES COUSTEAU.

The circle is an archetypical symbol: and the Earth itself is an orb; a sphere made of light, matter and energy; it is the sphere of all human existence. Within this sphere, throughout history there have been myriads of accounts of mysterious luminosities and light-forms; glowing spheres, angels, aliens, light beings and all kinds of anomalous lights; which have purposely interacted with individuals. Sometimes to the extent; that they have affected our beliefs and spiritual perceptions. Luminosities, whether spheres or light-forms; are part of human consciousness; they regularly appear in dreams, visions, altered states and paranormal experiences.

If we think of our own particular experience with luminosities and light-forms, which we've tried to view within the larger, worldwide context, there seems to be three main connecting factors: light, symbolism and consciousness.

By 'light' we mean both the electromagnetic energy frequency and all the visual paranormal phenomena similar to luminosities and light-forms within it.

By 'symbolism' we mean the common and archetypical meanings directly pertinent to the visual phenomena. By 'consciousness' we mean all those instances of apparent purpose, connectivity and synchronicity directly relative to our luminosities in particular, and to paranormal light phenomena in general.

Light, as we have seen, is fundamental to human existence, both at a biological and a spiritual level. What we have learned of Bio-photons qualifies this, showing us that our bodies, indeed all organic life forms, are transceivers; constantly collecting and radiating light. If we look at the whole of the organic world in that context, then, as humans, we are connected to a dynamic web of light that is constantly emitting and absorbing the light from the sun. It is a cyclical process.

Putting the notion of all organisms as transceivers of light; together with the concept of Earth as a sentient planetary bio-organism then we have what is essentially a sphere of light that contains consciousness! Could the luminosities, reported by so many throughout history be smaller spheres of consciousness?

Gustav Theodor Fechner, a 19th century doctor and professor of physics, who was one of the first professional academics to explore the possibility that plants had awareness; (later verified by the work of Cleve Backster) also put forward the notion that human life was made up of three stages: first; a continuous sleep from conception to birth; second; the half awake state we term as terrestrial existence; and third;

the fully aware state which begins only after death. Gustav Fechner, though scorned by many of his contemporaries, was a progressive thinker, and some of his speculations were of particular interest to us.

In his book, Comparative Anatomy of Angels, Fechner traced the evolution of consciousness through simple organisms, animals and humans to higher angelic beings, which he considered would be spherical in form and who would communicate not through sounds but through light itself, by luminous symbols! Now what could have possibly made him think that?

When we read this we had almost finished our book, but it was so pertinent to our own experience that we just had to briefly mention it here. There is a universality to the phenomena of luminosities which is more than mere coincidence.

Symbolically, the threefold combination of Light, Sphere and Consciousness, is in keeping with the universal concept of Oneness, symbolised by the circle, the sphere and the orb!

The concept of Oneness is perhaps almost perfectly expressed in the symbol of Tai Chi; where opposing cosmic principles are seen to make up a dynamic, interactive, and balanced circle of life. This could easily symbolise both Earth as seen in the Gaia Hypothesis; and Earth viewed as a Planetary Consciousness.

Whatever one may think of the idea of the Earth, not only as dynamic living super organism, but as a conscious entity, there is no doubt that circular symbols of Oneness have been with us since the dawn of time; and this very same symbolism is present in the luminosities and orbs photographed by us and many others.

The journey which for us began with orbs led us to the wider view of the Earth itself as a greater orb of planetary consciousness.

Looking back it seemed as though there was after all some

kind of progression in all our puzzling pixels. Basically it could be reduced to:

Small Transient Lights = Orbs = Luminosities = Light-Forms = Purpose.
Purpose = Consciousness = Primary Perception = Connectivity = GAIA.
GAIA = Living Organism = Consciousness!

Retrospectively it looked very much like someone was giving us great big hints drawn in images of light; the orbs and luminosities; pointedly symbolising Oneness! Together the concepts of GAIA, Primary Perception, synchronicity and the collective unconscious, give us the foundation for the connectivity of consciousness at all levels of our existence on this globe! The concepts of connectivity and Oneness; can be said to be perfectly symbolised by the circle, the sphere, the orb. Since the very beginning the luminosities had always given us much more to think about than just the photographs; and they hadn't finished yet!

LIGHT, ENERGY AND WATER
On 25 July we joined with people all over the world for the 'World Day of Love and Thanks to Water', inspired by the work of Dr Masaru Emoto, who in the spirit of the Gaia, Planetary Consciousness and the Primal Connectivity we have already touched on in the previous chapter, had initiated a method to connect with the Earth and try and purify polluted water by using the focussed positive thoughts and emotions of ordinary people. And amazingly against all accepted scientific views, it had worked.

Dr Emoto began his work in Japan and since then has extended it to many parts of the globe, where his annual ceremonies to cleanse and give thanks to water have drawn the concentrated thoughts of thousands towards this element that is so vital to our life and which covers almost three quarters of the earth's surface. Basically Dr Emotos' method is very simple; he gets people together to think positively about water, whether it is a glass of water, a pond, a lake or a river. Samples of water crystals have been taken before and after each ceremony; and the after samples consistently show improvements in the crystalline structure of water.

Amazingly polluted water, after being subjected to positive thoughts, has become less polluted! This fact shows very clearly that thought can affect matter.

It also indicates that human consciousness may be connected to a Gaian-type planetary consciousness. But in the context of what we'd learned about the luminosities this wasn't surprising! For if Gaia is real, if Primary Perception is real, if the collective unconscious and synchronicity are real; and we all are part of an interconnected living web of consciousness, why wouldn't it work?

On the day of the Water Ceremony at about 4.30 in the afternoon; we decided to go down to the stream and perform Masaru Emoto's simple positive thought ceremony there.

The ceremony involved putting your hands or fingers in the water; at the same time thinking about or saying out loud Dr Emoto's simple mantra of love, thanks and respect for water for a few minutes. Katie had all her thoughts on the ceremony and had not thought to bring her camera, but I had brought mine along, intending to document what we'd done. One of the shots taken that afternoon shows that a luminosity was also present. (Photo. 61.)

Perhaps it was empathising with what we are doing there?

Together we placed our fingers in the stream and concentrated on the mantra, then we thought about the cycle of water; how it arrived at

61

our home from the sea and clouds, how it fell as rain on the hills and ran down over the land and into our stream where it was now tricking through our fingers on its way back to the sea. We thought about all the life that the water touches on its way to the sea: fishes, birds, insects; and all the plants and trees that draw nutrients from the water. Along with all the creatures and animals that made up our beautiful world, we had water to thank for our existence. But as representatives of the human race, in our bit of Earth, we also had to say sorry too for the ignorance and greed of humans who have done so much damage to our seas and rivers. Concentrating our thoughts in this way felt very positive; we felt connected to the water.

Afterwards I wandered a little way up the bank, while Katie remained next to the stream; she wanted to feel the connection to the water for a little longer. When I turned back she was obviously still preoccupied with her meditation. It was at this point that I took a photograph of her, just to record what we'd done that day. While she was concentrating her thoughts on the water, Katie felt definite sensations which she later described in the following way:

"Suddenly my left hand tingled, returning my thoughts to the now. I remember thinking, was my hand cold from the fresh water, but my right hand felt warm, then opening my eyes, realised I only had my forefingers submerged."

The photograph I took of Katie, while she was busy meditating, with her fingertips in the stream, shows that there was also another presence. (Photo. 62.)

It clearly shows an unusual light-form. One that was definitely demonstrating an empathy with what we were doing there, because it was mimicking exactly what Katie was doing! We called this funny little light-form a 'water-sprite', because it does look a bit like a little elemental creature of light. Though whether; sprite; prana; an expression of planetary consciousness; or something else entirely; is open to question. But the fact was; that it was there and connected to the water!

Was this 'water sprite' another example of a living consciousness at work in our phenomena? We think it was for the following reasons:

1. It was preceded by the usual orb-like luminosity.
2. The 'sprite' appeared in the water on the very day of the water ceremony.
3. It is mimicking exactly what Katie is doing by sticking a part of itself in the water; almost as if saying: Yes, we are connected!

We have often questioned why we have been so privileged to photograph so many luminosities and light-forms. Perhaps it is simply because we have found them so enchanting? All we can hope to do with what we have is to try and communicate to others, through these images, that we share this world another consciousness.

An intelligence which; seems to be drawing our attention to the fact of its existence. But if, as we have previously questioned; our luminosities, and our cute little 'water-sprite' may be aspects of a planetary consciousness we may have more to consider than the feel good factor! There could be a much more serious side to such phenomena, if they are generated by a planetary consciousness.

As a living organism, the Earth, very much like the human brain, would appear, according to the GAIA concept; to be in touch with all its vital functions. And it is all too evident that we humans, like slugs in a cabbage patch, are gobbling up too many of the Earth's resources. Perhaps this has happened before?

According to the fossil record, palaeontology reveals the awful reality of many catastrophic extinction-level events. And here we come to another circular symbol: the symbol of Karma. We reap what we sow. As humans we don't let ants run riot in the pantry; and if the Earth is a super sentient organism, we ants could well be in danger of nibbling our way beyond the tolerance zone.

Perhaps instead of listening to the promises of politicians, which usually only amounts to either; 'put me in office' or 'keep me in office'; we need to be listening to those who are speaking for the Earth. Perhaps, like Dr Emoto, and others, we all need to be putting positive thought into action for our planet.

Whatever consciousness is behind the luminosities and light-forms, it has focussed our thoughts on humanity's connectivity to the Earth and its myriad life forms.

The whole spectrum of paranormal phenomena is pointless and futile if it has nothing to say to us about the basic issues of existence and consciousness.

Photographs of the paranormal, ours included; crop circles

and extrasensory perceptions of all kinds, are nothing in themselves; only signs pointing the way. Sure they are an expression of something Other - but they are not the something Other itself! Inherent in all paranormal phenomena, indeed, in phenomena of every kind, if we look carefully; is the question of: 'what is it that we are part of and what is it that we are?' Those are the really important issues for humanity!

In our journey through the previous pages, we have tried to go beyond the images, and the symbols, and take a peek at what is behind them. Perhaps it is now time to dispense with all the questions that have led us to this point and share with you what we ourselves have glimpsed in the enchanted realm behind the cloak of night.

CHAPTER 21

INFFINITY AND BEYOND

"Joy is not in things; it is within us."

RICHARD WAGNER

"It is good to have an end to journey towards; but it is the journey that matters in the end."

URSULA K. LE GUIN

So here we are at journeys end – almost. Like Bilbo Baggins we have travelled, "there and back again". And as you will probably recall, Bilbo had a circular door! But there's no need to worry; we're not going on a quest for circular symbolism in Middle-earth. Our journey through this one is quite enough to be going on with. We have pursued our orbs and luminosities in search of answers and along the way we've encountered Fireballs and Plasma Energies, Ghosts and Aliens, Star Signs and Symbols; not to mention Synchronicity and the Collective Unconscious. We have seen strange light-forms; and photographed faeries and Light Beings. Our quest for the meaning behind our phenomena has led us to, Chi Energy, Dolphins, Bio-photons and Primary Perception. From Crop Circles and Mandalas, we have turned with the Earth to see the world as GAIA, a living planetary organism; and from there we have seen the possibility of a planetary consciousness; connecting all life on Earth. Through celestial spheres, orbs and circular symbols we have discerned the Oneness of all things. We have learned that life may not be exactly as it seems; there is much more to discover.

In the film, 'Toy Story'; Buzz Lightyear discovered that he was not who he thought he was, and that he was part of a far different and larger world. Even though it was made as a children's entertainment, 'Toy Story', like many other good films, reflects the age old human quest for meaning. It seems amusingly ironic to us that the cry of, 'To infinity and beyond!' now comes out of the mouths of three and four year olds; for in terms of the individual human spirit, that may just about sum up where we are all heading. Whether teachers or pupils; scientists or paranormal investigators; we are all adventurers in a weird and wonderful universe.

Throughout history the luminosities and spheres that we have focussed on in this book have been recorded in woodcuts, tapestries, paintings and drawings. In the 19th century they were first captured on early photographs and cine-film, and then in the 20th century by camcorders. More recently, in the 21st century, orbs and luminosities have been photographed all over the world by digital cameras.

But it is not only on the Earth that strange luminosities have been recorded.

LUMINOSITIES BEYOND EARTH

Luminosities have also been videoed from space by NASA astronauts.

Various Space Shuttle missions have tracked and filmed inexplicable spheres and luminosities. For example: during the STS 80 Mission on 1 December 1996, shuttle astronauts filmed a large sphere rise up out of Earth's atmosphere and disappear into space. But by far the most intriguing pieces of footage we are aware of was taken by the STS 75 Shuttle Mission. This was the time when NASA had lost a hundred million dollar tethered satellite. Three days later they found the tether still attached to the satellite and the accompanying film of the recovery showed something quite amazing. All around the tether and the Shuttle were lots of spheres; myriads of them. They were of all sizes; moving in all directions, and rapidly changing direction, independently of each other.

To explain this, NASA offered up the ideas of space debris or ice crystals; but as all this was happening in low Earth orbit and subject to the Earth's gravitational field, it was transparently obvious that it was not physically possible for either debris or ice crystals to move independently of each other at different speeds to all points of the compass as these spheres did. The STS 75 footage shows them to be all over the place. No doubt some will see these spheres as alien spacecraft; but if you look carefully at the film, you can see that they don't look like craft at all. They behave more like a swarm of living creatures in air or water – like insects, jellyfish, microbes, or bacteria of varying sizes, all zipping about here, there and everywhere. Though the majority are mainly spherical, some of them are doughnut-like; and some seem to show motion trails or look like elongated ellipses. They are all constantly moving.

When we first saw this piece of NASA footage on a video about UFOs, we immediately saw similarities in the form and behaviour of these space spheres to the orbs and luminosities, which we and many others have been busily photographing here on Earth. Even though in scale they appear much larger than their Earthly counterparts; in form and by the way they rapidly move and change direction; these space spheres could just as equally be viewed as behaving like electrically driven plasma globes, or as organic life forms. They didn't look at all like flying saucers or nuts and bolts alien spacecraft; they behaved more like living entities!

We thought of all the accounts of orbs, luminosities, ball lightning and spheres that had been seen and photographed over the years by people all over the world.

All the connections we had made strongly indicated that the whole luminosity and light-form phenomena led back to one source; to the existence of a non-material, non-human consciousness; which though able to manifest itself visibly in our world was essentially an energy life-form. And judging by the STS 75 Shuttle footage, it seems that the non-material intelligence behind Earth based luminosities is also present in the higher atmosphere; and probably capable of travelling through space. In fact the Shuttle film shows that this is exactly what is happening in low Earth orbit, where spheres are seen moving through space.

How far they can travel beyond Earth we don't know. But we suspect quite a way.

We have used the term 'they' deliberately and whenever we have used the terms, 'intelligence' or 'consciousness' with reference to the luminosities/light-forms, we have meant it in the collective sense; even though we may not have said so at the time. So who are these space traversing luminosities? Where do they come from and what are they doing here?

All we can tell you is what our own experience and research has revealed and what our intuition or gut instincts tells us. You are naturally welcome to disagree with us. What follows is a summary of what we know, or believe so far, concerning the phenomena of luminosities and light-forms in general.

ONE: WHAT THEY ARE NOT

They are NOT: aliens, spirits of the dead, sprites, spirits of trees or faeries, though at times they have assumed all these forms; not to deliberately deceive us, but, we believe, to communicate. Very much like dolphins may mimic our behaviour; these entities empathise with us as individuals and to some extent may reflect our individual beliefs.

TWO: WHERE DO THEY COME FROM?

They come from Earth: or more specifically, from another aspect of reality centred here. This level of 'Other' reality where the luminosities/light-forms reside occupies the same space as we do; but unlike organic life forms, they don't exist solely in the universe of space, time and events. Unlike ourselves, who are, in effect, static beings, stuck within one frame of reference, the light-forms may exist in several realities at once. We have no reference points available to us with which to describe the reality continuum of the light-forms. All we can do is to study those areas where our reality touches theirs. These are the betwixt and between places where through mind, form, or spirit, we may at times connect with a wider consciousness. It is the overlapping of this Other reality with ours and the times of its direct connectivity to our level of consciousness that generates what we have come to view as paranormal phenomena.

THREE: WHAT ARE THEY?

All we can do here is to be totally speculative, because it is as impossible for humans to understand who, or what, these intelligences are as it would be for a dolphin to tell whether a human being was Greek or English, or whether a cow was different to a horse. Or more pertinently in terms of scale of consciousness: whether an ant could tell the difference between a cat, a giraffe or a human! Whether they are part of a planetary consciousness, or separate to it, we have no way of knowing, one way or the other. All we know is that, as far as our own consciousness and planetary environment is concerned; light-forms are symbiotic and empathic. It seems that in form and appearance here they are quite malleable, though we would suspect that their natural electro-physical form is the orb or sphere. But it also seems likely that light-forms may be able to assume any size from tiny points of light to glowing spheres many feet in diameter.

As the core environment of the light-forms is not bound by space or time, it would seem probable that they may well be as numerous as the stars in the sky. We believe that the consciousness which generates luminosities and light-forms exists both on and beyond Earth, and is endemic throughout the universe. In that context, although we have spoken of "they", in the sense of individual beings, we have to accept that our concept of individuation may not be remotely relevant to light-forms at all; except for their interactions at the human level. They may seem individuated to us, only because that is the way we are!

Light-forms are very difficult to define because they are so malleable to our perceptions. But what does seem quite relevant is their connectivity of consciousness with humans as individuals. It may well be that they are, after all, as individuated as we are; but at the same time totally connected to everything else. It is worth reflecting for a moment on the fact that though we are individual beings, our bodies are also transmitters and receivers of light. In one sense we operate much like a radio transceiver. In one sense we too are always connected to a universal environment; but just not aware of it!

It may be that light-forms, though individuated, may also be the means by which universal consciousness is radiated. In that sense light-forms could be seen by some as angelic messengers of light.

Could that be what people are seeing when they catch sight of Small Transient Light Phenomena – the visual signs of consciousness in action? If the Earth has a consciousness; and the luminosities are part of, or connected to it; then at times some humans may witness what is the equivalent, in planetary terms, to the electro-chemical activity of the mind.

FOUR: WHAT IS THEIR PURPOSE HERE?

In our own experience light-forms have appeared to be, enigmatic and yet playful; friendly but yet awe inspiring; a bit like a cross between a dolphin and an angel! As far as human beings are concerned the purpose of the light-forms is always filtered through our individuated perceptions. But whatever the individual interpretation; the over all message is always clearly an affirmation of an existence of a non-human consciousness.

If everyone knew that a higher non-human life form existed on Earth and that it was as real as we are, it would certainly change our perspective of reality.

FIVE: WHAT DOES THIS MEAN FOR HUMANITY?

Just as the butterfly emerges from the chrysalis to become a different kind of being from the caterpillar; it may be that we too change, and that from out of the physical form, Light Beings ascend to another level of existence.

We believe that light-forms are involved in the transformation of human consciousness. Behind all phenomena there is a universal process at work; at every level of existence there is change and transformation. Taken from a spiritual perspective, the dynamic ebb and flow of existence; as reflected in the symbol of Tai Chi, is a balance of opposites within Oneness. Everything we have learned of the luminosities and light-forms seems to qualify the connectivity of life and consciousness at every level.

Certainly this seems what all religion and psychology is striving towards; the spiritual unification of life and consciousness. But we do not believe this to be like a drop of water in the ocean – that is absorption, not connectivity.

True connectivity is that of a holistic community of individuals, balanced, harmonious, but individually aware. The symbol of Tai Chi shows the nature of true connectivity. Total Connection and Total Individuation! The two in one; Yin and Yang! Reading between the lines of the world beliefs and teachings inspired by the ever present luminosities and light-forms, it would seem that most major religions, though they may have lost the original meaning in the details, are essentially about a process of individual transformation leading to an integrated world in the Oneness of spirit!

Two thousand years ago, Jesus defined it simply enough for his followers: "Love your neighbour as yourself." In human terms this is the meaning of connectivity. Love as the connecting dynamic in relationships; not love as wishy-washy sentimentality. In order to love another as yourself you first have to love yourself. We cannot love what we do not know. Any knowing of the self requires true perception of the self. All that we own is who we are; but if all we think about is our self; we will diminish spiritually and there will be no spirit to rise into the light.

This is the spiritual journey that we are all on; and we ignore it at our peril.

Love is another aspect of Oneness. As any lover; or believer of any faith will testify; love is transformative; which is obviously why it is such a central part of most spiritual teachings throughout history.

According to some, the one other creature, apart from humans, which seems to evidence spiritual qualities, is the dolphin. If we could ask dolphins what they think human activities in their oceans and human contact with their species may mean, and what may be the purpose behind it all; I wonder what their reply would be? Is the intrusion of our technology into their environment as inexplicable to them as paranormal phenomenon is to us? But whatever it means to them, they know that we exist – and that our existence impinges on their lives; and vice versa. We too now live within the context of a sea- going life form that is at least as intelligent as we are. Human contact with dolphins may go some way to help us get a perspective on humanities contact with higher, non-human intelligences; which may 'dive' into our environment in very similar fashion to which we explore the oceans. In terms of trying to understand what we are part of, both dolphins and light-forms offer us the opportunity for a new perspective on the cosmos.

AT THE EDGE OF IMMENSITIES:

We don't think that it is any coincidence that in the first half of this new millennium the incidence of precognition and empathic abilities, are becoming more wide spread; nor that the occurrence of orbs, luminosities and light beings is also increasing. Could something be happening? People all over the world are feeling a heightened sense of spiritual affinity with the Earth; and it seems quite synchronistic that in spite of all the troubles on our world, thousands of people, of all faiths and beliefs are looking outward with a sense of expectancy. Somewhere, at some level; we all can feel it at times. Change is coming. Some look for a change imposed from the outside, but spiritually all real change begins within the self. We have had it spelled out to us in all the major beliefs and faiths of the world. Love others as you love yourself. The Kingdom of heaven is within you! We must change our perceptions before we can change the world. The problem is that we humans live in a divided reality: without Oneness. In the human world man is divided from himself and divided from others of his kind; he is divided from other species and also from the world around him. This is the negative side of individuation. But subconsciously, we are impelled to seek for connectivity, within our selves, with each other, with other beings and with the Earth. The concept of the circle, the orb; the ideal of Oneness is ingrained in our psyche.

The unification of faiths, political unity, the scientific search for a unified theory, even our current preoccupation of needing to be in contact all the time; by internet; by email, by mobile phones: all these are the expression of some deep spiritual need within us. We need to be connected – but we also need our individuation to realise that connection; to perceive it, to affirm it, and to enjoy it! It is at this level that luminosities and light-forms speak to the spirit within us; to that which is more than the body that holds it.

In as many guises as there are individuals, these non-human intelligences have spoken to us throughout our history. Their symbols and forms are rooted in the collective unconscious of humanity; their message of Oneness is echoed in temples and churches; studied by psychologists, seen in crop circles and illuminated by the stars. Somewhere, at some level, we all know we are part of something more. Today, as the world is changing around us, voices from all beliefs tell us that we are not living in ordinary times.

Those with their senses tuned to psychic frequencies; can sense some thing in the air! Some speak of coming transformation; a psychic shift of consciousness; is this all just wishful thinking? Or are we, like Buzz Lightyear, about to find that we are part of far greater Reality; one which takes us to infinity and beyond?

In a very real sense we are.

Our Earth moves around the sun at around 107,000 kilometres per hour; and as the great orb of the sun pulls our solar system around the immense wheel of the galaxy it is moving through space at roughly, 900,000 kilometres per hour; and even at that speed, it takes the sun over 220 million years to make one complete revolution of the galaxy! The Earth and everything on it, is literally never in the same space for more than a second or two! We are continually moving at incredible speeds, along with billions of other stars and galaxies through a universe so vast it is almost beyond comprehension! So are we caught up in a greater reality? Yes, we are! But that is only the physical universe; and as huge and awe inspiring as that is; the universe of consciousness is immensely larger!

Consciousness, like energy, extends unseen through all levels of existence; divided into countless trillions of parts, which are themselves divided into billions of parts. One of those parts of which there are billions upon billions of that specific type is a consciousness which can detect the smallest changes in light and sound; it has the ability to learn, to process information and communicate knowledge; it can accurately measure the polarisation of sunlight; it is sensitive to electro-magnetic fields and can use them for guidance whilst flying at incredible speeds and performing amazingly accurate pinpoint manoeuvres. It can do all this and at the same time keep constant track of time by the use of a brain that is no bigger than a grain of sand. We know this consciousness as a bee!

The individual brains which contain our human consciousness are ten million times larger and billions of times more complex. And yet we are only but one species within the ecosphere of a huge living bio-organism that is teaming with billions of seen and unseen conscious beings at every level. Some of which physically are so small they outnumber us billions to one; and some of which by contrast with us are so vastly different to us in terms of form and consciousness that by contrast, we ourselves are like the ants in our own gardens.

The luminosities and light-forms had taught us one thing; that we, all of us, are part of a wider environment. Like little ants peering over the edge of immensities, thinking humans all over the world are wondering, what we are and where we are going – if that knowledge affects our ultimate future; if like the caterpillar we are destined to be something else – then we'd better find out!

While we are each preoccupied with our small concerns, our little garden world is moving with the stars in their courses through the vastness of existence. Perhaps it is even now moving out of one cosmic season into another! Perhaps a season of change is coming?

Far away the orbs and luminosities that are distant stars shine in the depths of space, revolving in the immensity of infinity, beyond the comprehension of Buzz Lightyear, or the ants in our gardens. Here on the living bio-organism of Earth, people crawl over the surface fighting tiny wars with tiny minds, oblivious to the immensities that surround them. As our scientists peer down microscopes at swarming microbes; who are totally ignorant of our existence; somewhere in the unknown; on a level of consciousness vastly different to ours; other intelligences, in turn study us.

We have come, not to the end, but to a new beginning! And before we journey on we have two last photographs to share with you.

The first: Photo CP1, was taken not by a digital camera but by my old SLR Pentax MV1, in the spring of 2004. For me it captures the enchantment of our lights and orbs phenomena. The second: Photo CP7, was taken in our garden one evening as this book was being written. Like most of our images it was shot with our digital camera. What you see here is exactly as it appeared to us. From orbs to light beings the phenomenon is on going.

Out of the dark they come – spheres, luminosities, light-forms; like angel messengers writing in symbols of light! Something is happening – just a glimmer; a twinkle; a flash of light! Something different – something Other!

You are not alone! And if we are right; they are right next to you, right now!

There is only One. And the One is the Many.

Formless and Formed; Spirit and Matter; Light and Dark.

You and Me. In Each is the All. And All are the One!

PHOTOGRAPHING LUMINOSITIES:

For those interested in photographing Luminosities,
here are some questions and answers

Q: *Which digital camera should I use to photograph orbs?*
A: It doesn't matter, any camera will do, but we'd advise against using one make of camera exclusively – get a friend to join you and photograph you with theirs, or vice versa; or you could get an inexpensive second camera to take comparison shots.

Q: *Do I need a camera with 20x digital zoom facility?*
A: No! In fact avoid using digital zoom, you only need 3x upwards optical zoom.

A good Optical zoom does not degrade the image.

When out taking photographs of luminosities and light-forms we never use the digital zoom facility because digital zoom tends to degrade the image too much.

Shots taken outdoors at night will vary according to lighting conditions.

If the conditions are too dark you may have to lighten the image quite considerably in order to see what you have. This can often result in problems with image quality.

Using Digital zoom can degrade image quality from the outset.

Q: *Why are some images more grainy than others?*
A: This is usually due to lighting conditions when taking the shot and to the amount the image was lightened or enhanced on the computer afterwards.

When we first began to photograph orbs and light-forms, we had no thought as to reproduction, or to writing a book. All we were concerned with initially was to lighten or enhance the image to clearly see what exactly was there on the digital photo.

This often resulted in loss of detail in some of the images. At the time we were not saving originals but we later learned that it made good sense to save the originals.

Q: *What is the best way to optimise the quality of the luminosity or light-form?*
A: The best way is to first save the original image, untouched. Then make a copy and use Adobe Photoshop to lighten and/or enhance. If our own images merited it we'd sometimes we'd do three or four comparative versions of the same image: lightening, darkening and enhancing; using Photoshop's Unsharp Mask, Curves, and Hue and Saturation tools. But be careful; lightening an image too much can result in obliterating detail from the subject matter. After a few mistakes we learned to strike a balance between best visibility of the luminosities and the over all reproduction quality of the image.

Q: *What is the best time of night to photograph luminosities?*
A: In our experience, just after dusk, when the night is not yet totally dark, is the best time to photograph luminosities and light-forms.

Q: *How can I be sure that what I'm photographing are genuine luminosities, not natural phenomena; such as dust, pollen or insects?*
A: Being aware of possible natural causes in the first place will help you to avoid and recognise them. For example; as a general rule, we would advise against taking shots in the rain, or in humid or misty conditions, as it may be possible that water droplets may reflect

in the flash.

We would advise any would-be orb photographer to choose conditions that minimise the possibility of atmospheric related effects.

Anyone trying to photograph luminosities and light-forms should consider all obvious natural causes of odd effects and try to minimise the likely hood of these occurring by choosing times and places where they are less likely.

Q: *Which places are more likely for photographing luminosities?*
A: Because luminosities are ubiquitous, you can never be totally sure, but some places do seem to attract them more than others. As a general rule though, we'd suggest that you return to places where you have already photographed odd light phenomenon, and frequently take shots in those places. Genuine luminosities will respond to your visits and to your intentionality, often confirming their presence by increased photo-interactivity and sometimes by relating to you as an individual.

Q: *How can I be sure that I'll be able to photograph luminosities?*
A: You can't, but once you've got one, you'll get more. However, there is a way to increase your odds. If you or someone you know, sees Small Transient Lights phenomena (STL) then you can use occurrences of that phenomena as a guide to the most likely direction to point your camera. Whether indoors or outside, in daylight or at night, the chances are that if you see STLs, then luminosities are not far away; and if you're quick enough and persistent enough, sooner or later you are sure to photograph something that is, in one sense, beyond photography!

Bibliography and References:

The Authors wish to thank and acknowledge the authors and publishers of the references used in the preparation of this book and to recommend them, and the other books listed below, for further reading.

Astronomy:

The Intelligent Universe, by Fred Hoyle. Michael Joseph Ltd.

A History of Astronomy, by Anton Pannekoek. George Allen.

The Cosmic Connection, by Carl Sagan. Doubleday.

Science and Theory:

The Tao Of Physics, by Fritjof Capra Fontana/Collins.

The Faber Book of Science, edited By John Carey. Faber and Faber.

A portrait of Isaac Newton, by E. Frank Manuel.
   New Republic Books.

Betrayers of the Truth, by William Broad & Nicholas Wade.
   Century Publishing.

Consciousness and Psychology:

JUNG Selected Writings, Fontana Original.

The Practical Use of Dream-Analysis, (1934).

Synchronicity: An Acausal Connecting Principle. (1952).

The Language of Symbols, by David Fontana, Duncan Baird
   Publishers.

The Cognitive Unconscious, by J.F. Kihlstrom
   Science, no: 237:1445–1452.

The Roots of Coincidence, by Arthur Koestler. Pan Books.

Dreams and Dreaming, by Tony Crisp. London House.

The Psychology of Perception, by M.D. Vernon. Penguin Books Ltd.

Earth and Living Organisms:

Gaia, by J. Lovelock. Oxford University Press.

Gaia the Growth of an Idea, by Lawrence E. Joseph. Penguin.

Oasis in Space, by Jacques Cousteau. Angus & Robertson (U.K.).

The Secret Life of Plants, by Peter Tompkins & Christopher Bird.
    Penguin.

The Dolphin Cousin to Man, by Robert Stenuit. Pelican Books.

The Magic of the Senses, by Vitus B. Droscher. Granada Publishing.

Creationism Revisited, by Dr Colin Mitchell. Autumn House Ltd.

Light and Energy:

The Healing Energies of Light, by Roger Coghill. Gaia Books.

The Energy of Life, by Guy Brown. Harper Collins Publishers.

UFOs and Aliens:

The UFO Encyclopedia, by Margaret Sachs. Transworld Publishers.

Uninvited Visitors, by Ivan T. Sanderson. Neville Spearman Ltd.

Dimensions, by Jacques Vallee. Macdonald & Co. (Publishing) Ltd.

Passport to the Cosmos, by Dr. John E. Mack. Harper Collins.

Alien Dawn by Colin Wilson. Virgin Publishing Ltd.

Alien Investigator, by Tony Dodd. Headline Book Publishing.

Ancient Beliefs:

Ancient Myths, by Rudolf Steiner. Steiner Book Centre, Toronto.

The Ancient Science of Geomancy, by N. Pennick. Thames &
    Hudson. 1979.

Feng-Shui, by E.J. Eitel. Synergetic Press edition. 1984.
Native American Myth & Legend, by Mike Dixon-Kennedy. Blanford.
Burning Water, by Laurette SéJourné. Thames and Hudson.
Highland Fairy Legends, by James Macdougall. D. S. Brewer. Ltd.

Crop Circles:
Crop Circles, by Carolyn North. Ronin Publishing, Inc.
Circular Evidence, by Pat Delgado & Colin Andrews.
    Guild Publishing London.

Paranormal Phenomena & the Supernatural:
The Book of Charles Fort, by Charles Fort. Henry Holt & Co., 1941.
Earthlights, by P. Devereux. Turnstone Press. 1982.
The Paranormal, by Stan Gooch Fontana 1979.
Elements of Psychophysics. By Gustav Theodor Fechner. Holt,
    Rinehart & Winston. New York 1966.
Ghosts, edited by Morven Eldritch Geddes and Grosset.
Super Natural England, edited by Betty Puttick. Countryside Books.
The Unexplained, (Complete Part Work). Orbis Publishing Ltd.
How to Read the Aura, by W. E. Butler. The Aquarian Press. 1979.
Life After Life, by Ramond. A. Moody Jr. Bantam.
The After Death Experience, by Ian Wilson. Transworld.

Miscellaneous Reference:
You Get Brighter, a song, by The Incredible String Band.
Readers Digest Universal Dictionary.
An Index of Possibilities, Clanose Publishers 1974.
Tree and Leaf, by J.R.R. Tolkien. George Allen and Unwin.

Websites:

Lucy Pringle's Crop Circle site

UFO Document Index

Dr Masaru Emoto. www.thank-water.net

Nexus Magazine. www.nexusmagazine.com

orbstudy.com

www.o-books.net

www.lights2beyond.com

Credits for illustrations and pictures:

All photographs are copyright of the authors, unless specified otherwise. Although every effort has been made to trace the owners of other copyright illustrations and pictures used in this book, this has not always been possible.

Page: 74. Woodcuts Fig. B. and Fig. C.
Wickiana Collection Zurich Library

Page: 90. Fireball at Basle. 1907 Photo: M. Bessy.

Page: 176. Fig. J. Christ in the clouds. Korea 1950s Keystone Press.

O

is a symbol of the world,
of oneness and unity. O Books
explores the many paths of wholeness
and spiritual understanding which
different traditions have developed down
the ages. It aims to bring this knowledge
in accessible form, to a general readership,
providing practical spirituality to today's seekers.

For the full list of over 200 titles covering:

- CHILDREN'S PRAYER, NOVELTY AND GIFT BOOKS
  - CHILDREN'S CHRISTIAN AND SPIRITUALITY
    - CHRISTMAS AND EASTER
      - RELIGION/PHILOSOPHY
        - SCHOOL TITLES
      - ANGELS/CHANNELLING
      - HEALING/MEDITATION
    - SELF-HELP/RELATIONSHIPS
    - ASTROLOGY/NUMEROLOGY
      - SPIRITUAL ENQUIRY
    - CHRISTIANITY, EVANGELICAL
      AND LIBERAL/RADICAL
      - CURRENT AFFAIRS
      - HISTORY/BIOGRAPHY
    - INSPIRATIONAL/DEVOTIONAL
    - WORLD RELIGIONS/INTERFAITH
      - BIOGRAPHY AND FICTION
      - BIBLE AND REFERENCE
      - SCIENCE/PSYCHOLOGY

Please visit our website,
www.O-books.net

Let The Standing Stones Speak

Messages from the Archangels revealed

Natasha Hoffman with Hamilton Hill

The messages encoded in the standing stones of Carnac in Brittany, France, combine and transcend spiritual truths from many disciplines and traditions, even though their builders lived thousands of years before Buddha, Christ and MuhammAd. The revelations received by the authors as they read the stones make up a New Age Bible for today.

"an evergreen..a permanent point of reference for the serious seeker."
IAN GRAHAM, author of *God is Never Late*

Natasha Hoffman is a practising artist, healer and intuitive, and lives with her partner Hamilton in Rouziers, France.

1-903816-79-3
£9.99 $14.95

Is There An Afterlife?

David Fontana

The question whether or not we survive physical death has occupied the minds of men and women since the dawn of recorded history. The spiritual traditions of both West and East have taught that death is not the end, but modern science generally dismisses such teachings.

The fruit of a lifetime's research and experience by a world expert in the field, *Is There An Afterlife?* presents the most complete survey to date of the evidence, both historical and contemporary, for survival of physical death. It looks at the question of what survives-personality, memory, emotions and body image-in particular exploring the question of consciousness as primary to and not dependent on matter in the light of recent brain research and quantum physics. It discusses the possible nature of the afterlife, the common threads in Western and Eastern traditions, the common features of "many levels," group souls and reincarnation.

As well a providing the broadest overview of the question, giving due weight to the claims both of science and religion, *Is There An Afterlife?* brings it into personal perspective. It asks how we should live in this life as if death is not the end, and suggests how we should change our behaviour accordingly.

David Fontana is a Fellow of the British Psychological Society (BPS), Founder Chair of the BPS Transpersonal Psychology Section, Past President and current Vice President of the Society for Psychical Research, and Chair of the SPR Survival Research Committee. He is Distinguished Visiting Fellow at Cardiff University, and Professor of Transpersonal Psychology at Liverpool John Moores University. His many books on spiritual themes have been translated into 25 languages.

1 903816 90 4
£11.99/$16.95

Past Life Angels
Discovering Your Life's Master-plan
Jenny Smedley
Everyone knows about the existence of Angels, but this book reveals the discovery of a very special and previously unsuspected legion- that of Past Life Angels. These beings are not only here and now; they have been with us through all our lives, since our soul's creation. They are still there to nudge us, guide us and jog our memories. The clues are there, and by following them we can kick our higher self into operation, and change our lives beyond recognition.

When we connect with our Past Life Angels we no longer drift through life uncertain of who we really are and what we should be doing. Our instincts are right-our lives are unfinished business. Our soul is eternal, and has a job to do in this life. It has a master plan that has evolved through all our lifetimes.

For the first time, *Jenny Smedley* shows why your past lives are important to your future and how they can change your current one. She discusses the contracts made before this birth, both with others and yourself. She explains the illnesses and fears we suffer from, and, above all, how we can stick to the right path with the help of our Past Life Angels, once we have found it.

Waste no more time on your spiritual path, read this book and be inspired, awakened and ready to run where others walk; I wish it were around when I was ignoring those nudges and stumbling through life's lessons!
DAVID WELLS, Astrologer and Medium

Jenny Smedley has done it again and created an excellent book which helps you in this life, and the next. I work with my own angels every day but this book has shown me a new avenue to explore. Learn how your angels can hep you with your current life challenges using the assistance of your past life angels. Jenny certainly knows her stuff, and her many fans will not be disappointed.
JACKY NEWCOMB, angel teacher, columnist, presenter and author of *An Angel Treasury*

Jenny Smedley, columnist and writer, has condensed ten years experience and research into this book. A guest speaker on hundreds of radio and TV shows worldwide, she wrote it in response to the many requests she gets on how we can find that *something* that's missing from our lives.

1 905047 31 2
£9.99/$16.95

Journey Home

Tonika Rinar

Tonika Rinar believes that everybody is capable of time travel. We can access history as it really happened, without later exaggeration or bias. We can also heal ourselves by coming to terms with our experiences in past lives.

Tonika escorts the reader into other worlds and dimensions, explaining her own remarkable experiences with an easy-to-read approach. At one level the book can simply be taken as a series of fascinating experiences with the paranormal, embracing past life regression, ghosts, angels and spirit guides. But it also encourages the reader along their own journey of self-discovery and understanding. A journey in which you can discover your own connection with the Universe and the many different dimensions contained within Creation.

Journey Home offers a multitude of insights, and along the way looks at some of the fundamental questions asked by all cultures around the world. Where do we come from? Why are we here? What is the point of our life? What happens when we die?

Tonika Rinar is an extraordinary psychic and visionary, international speaker and workshop leader, with 17 years clinical experience in working with people suffering injury and illness. She has been interviewed extensively on radio and TV.

1 905047 00 2
£11.99 $16.95

Torn Clouds

Judy Hall

Drawing on thirty years experience as a regression therapist and her own memories and experiences in Egypt, ancient and modern, *Torn Clouds* is a remarkable first novel by an internationally-acclaimed MBS author, one of Britain's leading experts on reincarnation. It features time-traveller Megan

McKennar, whose past life memories thrust themselves into the present day as she traces a love affair that transcends time. Haunted by her dreams, she is driven by forces she cannot understand to take a trip to Egypt in a quest to understand the cause of her unhappy current life circumstances. Once there, swooning into a previous existence in Pharaonic Egypt, she lives again as Meck'an'ar, priestess of the Goddess Sekhmet, the fearful lion headed deity who was simultaneously the Goddess of Terror, Magic and Healing.

Caught up in the dark historical secrets of Egypt, Megan is forced to fight for her soul. She succeeds in breaking the curse that had been cast upon her in two incarnations.

Judy Hall is a modern seer who manages the difficult task of evoking the present world, plus the realm of Ancient Egypt, and making them seem real. There is an energy behind the prose, and a power in her imagery which hints that this is more than just a story of character and plot, but an outpouring from another age, a genuine glimpse into beyond-time Mysteries which affect us all today.
ALAN RICHARDSON, author of *Inner Guide to Egypt.*

Judy Hall has been a karmic counsellor for thirty years. Her books have been translated into over fourteen languages.

1 903816 80 7
£9.99/$14.95

The Vision
Out-of-body revelations of divine wisdom
Jaap Hiddinga
Visions and out-of-body experiences are not uncommon, but few have been experienced in such depth, and articulated with such clarity, as those of *Jaap Hildinga*. He began to have them as a young child, and out of the

thousands he has accumulated since then he presents here some of the most powerful. They range from the Christ awareness that came into the world at the birth of Jesus to travels in other dimensions, in other times, in this universe and beyond. Along the way he raises questions and suggests answers about the origins of Christianity, the nature of the quantum world, the links between the earthly and spiritual worlds, and the future of humanity

Jaap Hildinga offers no particular interpretation or path to wisdom. It is not a book on how to travel out of the body, but a record of what one person was shown when he did so. The visions are recorded as they were received. As he says, each individual can take from it what they want or need. His conviction is that they can be of value to other searchers. They changed his life, maybe they can change yours. They point to a universe that is lovingly shepherding humanity to a future that at present it can barely dream of.

Jaap Hildinga studied chemistry at university and set up a petrochemical engineering firm at Falkirk in Scotland, where he has lived for the last twenty years. In 1993 he had a revelation that completely changed his thinking and his way of life. He sold the company he had set up, and is now an independent advisor for management and export marketing.

£9.99/$14.95

1 905047 05 3

The 7 Aha!s of Highly Enlightened Souls

Mike George

With thousands of insights now flooding the market place of spiritual development, how do we begin to decide where to start our spiritual journey? What are the right methods? This book strips away the illusions that surround the modern malaise we call stress. In 7 insights, it reminds us of the essence of all the different paths of spiritual wisdom. It succinctly describes what we need to realize in order to create authentic happiness and live with greater contentment. It finishes with the 7 AHA!S, the "eureka moments", the practice of any one of which will profoundly change your life in the most positive way.

Mike George is a spiritual teacher, motivational speaker, retreat leader and management development facilitator. He brings together the three key strands of his millennium-spiritual and emotional intelligence, leadership development, and continuous learning. His previous books include *Discover Inner Peace, Learn to Relax* and *In The Light of Meditation.*

1 903816 31 9
£5.99 $11.95

Humming Your Way to Happiness

An introduction to Tuva and Overtone singing from around the world
Peter Galgut
Ancient peoples have always used incantations and music to tune into nature and achieve expanded consciousness, better health, and for purposes of divination. The most powerful of all forms of sound healing and transformation is the technique of overtone chant, still practiced in many parts of the world today.

This guide shows you how to calm and focus the mind through singing the ancient way. It draws on sources from around the world, covering Pythagorean, Eastern, Jewish, Christian, American and African musical traditions. It covers ancient beliefs in the Lost Chords, Music of the Spheres, Tantras, Chakras, the Kabbalistic tree as well as modern concepts of white sound, brainwave generation and others. It is full of techniques and tips on how to keep "on top", using sound, music and harmony, helping you to take control of your life in your own way in your own time.

Dr Peter Galgut is a medical scientist and clinician at London University, as well as a qualified Acupuncturist and Homeopath.

1 905047 14 2
£9.99 $16.95

Bringing God Back to Earth
John Hunt

Religion is an essential part of our humanity. We all follow some form of religion, in the original meaning of the word. But organised religion establishes definitions, boundaries and hierarchies which the founders would be amazed by. If we could recover the original teachings and live by them, we could change ourselves and the world for the better. We could bring God back to earth.

"The best modern religious book I have read. A masterwork."
ROBERT VAN DE WEYER, author of *A World Religions Bible.*
"Answers all the questions you ever wanted to ask about God and some you never even thought of."
RICHARD HOLLOWAY, former Primus Episcopus and author of *Doubts and Loves.*

John Hunt runs a publishing company of which **O Books** is an imprint.

1-903816-81-5
£9.99 $14.95